# Gardening Lunar Lore

## Planting with the Moon

Published by My Spirit Books 2013

First published in Great Britain in 2013 by My Spirit Books,
Maidstone TV Studio,
Vinters Park, Maidstone, Kent ME14 5NZ
www.myspiritbooks.com

Cover design by Robert Hammond

Printed and bound in the UK by Berforts

British Library Cataloguing-in-Publication Data
A catalogue record for this book is available on request from the
British Library

ISBN:
978-1-908810-36-6 Paperback
978-1-908810-37-3 Kindle
978-1-908810-38-0 Ebook

# Contents

Introduction                                                    1

Part One                                                        5

        Lunar Activity Guide                7

        Lunar Gardening Lore              21

        Void-of-Course Moon              31

        General Weather                    41
        Expectations

Part Two                                                       57

        January                            59

        February                           67

        March                              75

        April                              83

        May                                91

        June                               99

        July                              107

        August                            115

        September                         123

        October                           131

        November                          139

        December                          147

Tips and Wrinkles                                             155

# Introduction

✺

*The Gardening Year*

This really is a misnomer of a title if ever there was one, because for the ardent gardener there is no start or finish, it is just one long — very long — period of incessant hard work.

And even if people use astrological knowledge to help them achieve better results, while it may ease the load somewhat, the pressure is never really very far away. Admittedly, all this is likely to be swept aside when the results come through.

Beds of colourful flowers, bushes and trees brimming with fruit, their yield a tribute to the time spent nurturing them. Then there are the vegetable growths to be appreciated as row upon row of edible and tasty additions to meals spring forth. And who can pass by lush green lawns to admire while others lounge on garden furniture perhaps spread around sparkling ponds and rockeries?

Well, that is one view.

There are a few people, admittedly not many, who have a natural gift for gardening. "Green fingers" is the usual term. It denotes those who seem to have only to touch this or dig that and a few weeks later — perfect results.

## Why astrology and gardening?

For many years, centuries actually, these two disciplines have been inextricably linked in that farmers and gardeners have been sowing, planting, cultivating and gathering in their various growths in tune with the signs of the zodiac or, to be more precise, when the Moon is known to have been in this or that sign.

There are those who speak of leaf, flower, root and fruit days and of planting or sowing this or that when the Moon is transiting (passing through) a particular sign. Many are not totally aware of why, because of the way this knowledge has been passed down through the ages, but it offers excellent results.

Through the years I've found these four basic terms seem to either cloud the issue or make it hard for the ordinary person to understand. I will explain them so that you may experiment, but I prefer when and where to do what and when as the Moon passes through this or that sign and, most importantly, what phase she is in at that time.

Leaf days are when the Moon is transiting or passing through Cancer, Scorpio or Pisces, also known as the water signs. It is suggested that these are the best times to plant out or sow vegetables like cabbage, lettuce or other plants noted their leaf foods.

Flower days are when the Moon is in Aries, Leo or Sagittarius, also known as the fire signs. It has been recommended that these are the best days to sow or plant out cauliflowers, broccoli and so on.

Root days are when the Moon is passing through Taurus, Virgo or Capricorn, also known as the earth signs. When the Moon is here one should deal with plants that supply food that grow in the ground like potatoes, parsnips and carrots.

Fruit days are associated with Gemini, Libra or Aquarius, the air signs, and it is suggested these times are when you should concentrate on planting or sowing tomatoes, peas and beans.

A more complete understanding of what exercise to pursue at any given time is explained in the chapter called *Astrological Lunar Lore* while in the *Lunar Activity Guide* pages you will find all the usual plants we might normally associate with gardening along with the best times for when and how you should pursue such things.

Now you can join that happy band of people simply by observing the astrological hints given for each month. However, you must also try to remember that the weather indicators are usually presented in or have to be in a widely general form. There is rarely enough space to localise this information. For those seriously interested, there are books available that specialise in weather forecasting using lunar and planetary lore.

However, let us return to gardening lunar lore. Please note that all vegetables, fruits and plants mentioned for one activity or another throughout this book are referred to with their most astrologically appropriate lunar time and sign for the reader to plant or sow.

You are also reminded that up until now you would have been asked to use a good gardening guide for the proper season and best month in which to actually start the plant or growths concerned. As much information as possible has been has been included in the relevant chapter in respect of the month concerned, and you will find that you can cross reference these exercises with other plants of a similar nature.

A word of caution perhaps might also be helpful at this stage. It is not always possible to follow the advice given in the ensuing pages for one reason or another, especially where the weather is concerned. This is why space has been allowed to outline the average expectations for each month.

A chapter on astrological weather forecasting has been included, for in this country so much depends on what does happen not just in our gardening worlds, but also in the greater farming communities. Alternative times for many activities have been included for just such occasions.

The work listed here to be undertaken during each month is far from complete, because this book is meant as a general guide. Where a task is advised that you try to time your efforts with either the phase of the Moon or its position to do this or that on a particular day is not complete either.

A task or tip not being mentioned in either category does not mean you should not pursue such work. It simply means it hasn't been included.

However, there is one golden rule to observe, even if you are not an astrological gardener. One should never start or try to finish any activity or task under a "void-of-course" Moon for nothing ever goes right at such times.

I have included a complete explanation of what a void-of-course Moon is and what to expect when it does happen.

Happy gardening.

# Part One

# Lunar Activity Guide

This chapter concerns itself with the when and how of planting and sowing vegetables, flowers, fruit trees, bushes, herbs, and all other garden growths and activities. Where possible, I have tried to list what I can in respect of everything one might encounter while in the average garden, but (as with all things) the list is not complete. Something not being mentioned doesn't mean you cannot undertake the task.

Thus, the majority of plants, vegetables and fruits are listed along with the best period, phase (or quarter) of the Moon. Also shown is the best time for which sign the Moon passes through for such activities. Sometimes you will find that a sign is suggested that may not agree with the Moon phase of the moment or, vice versa, it implies a phase that may seem out of kilter with the sign the Moon occupies.

What is important is that all these recommendations have been checked and what is here are the most favoured signs and times for planting or sowing for each month of the gardening year.

For example, as an astrological guide a good period, although not necessarily for the first time in the year, one should sow broccoli or cauliflower during the first week of March. The list recommends one should wait for the

Moon to be in the first quarter and transiting (or passing through) Cancer, Libra, Scorpio or Pisces for the best results. However, it is possible that the Moon may be in a position for this or that to be sown or planted a week earlier or later. Be guided accordingly.

**Fruit and vegetables**

| Plant | Phase | Sign |
|---|---|---|
| Annuals | 1 or 2 | Libra |
| Apple tree | 3 | Taurus, Cancer, Sagittarius, Pisces |
| Apricot tree | 2 or 3 | Taurus, Libra, Capricorn |
| Artichoke (both types) | 1 | Taurus, Cancer, Virgo, Pisces |
| Asparagus | 1 | Cancer, Scorpio, Pisces |
| Aubergine | 2 | Cancer, Libra, Scorpio, Pisces |
| Barley | 1 or 2 | Cancer, Libra, Capricorn, Pisces |
| Beans | 2 | Taurus, Cancer, Libra, Pisces |
| Beech tree | 2 or 3 | Capricorn |
| Beetroot | 3 | Cancer, Libra, Scorpio, Capricorn, Pisces |
| Bramble fruit | 2 | Cancer, Scorpio, Pisces |

| Plant | Phase | Sign |
| --- | --- | --- |
| Broccoli | 1 | Cancer, Libra, Scorpio, Pisces |
| Blackberry | 2 | Cancer, Scorpio, Pisces |
| Brussels sprouts | 1 | Cancer, Libra, Scorpio, Pisces |
| Bulbs | 3 | Cancer, Scorpio, Pisces |
| Bulbs for seed | 2 or 3 | Taurus, Cancer, Libra, Scorpio, Pisces |
| Cabbage | 1 | Taurus, Cancer, Libra, Scorpio, Pisces |
| Carrot | 3 | Cancer, Libra, Scorpio, Pisces |
| Cauliflower | 1 | Taurus, Cancer, Libra, Scorpio, Pisces |
| Celeriac | 3 | Cancer, Scorpio, Pisces |
| Celery | 1 | Taurus, Libra, Capricorn |
| Cherry tree | 2 or 3 | Cancer, Scorpio, Pisces |
| Chicory | 2 or 3 | Cancer, Scorpio, Pisces |
| Clover | 1 or 2 | Cancer, Scorpio, Pisces |

| Plant | Phase | Sign |
|---|---|---|
| Corn | 1 | Cancer, Libra, Scorpio, Pisces |
| Courgettes | 2 | Cancer, Scorpio, Pisces |
| Cress | 1 | Cancer, Scorpio, Pisces |
| Cucumber | 1 | Cancer, Virgo, Libra, Scorpio, Pisces |
| Deciduous trees | 2 or 3 | Water or air signs |
| Endive | 1 | Cancer, Virgo, Libra, Scorpio, Pisces |
| Evergreen trees | 2 or 3 | Taurus, Libra |
| Fig tree | 2 or 3 | Taurus, Cancer, Virgo, Libra, Scorpio, Pisces |
| Flowers (general) | 1 or 2 | Scorpio, Sagittarius |
| Garlic | 1 or 2 | Cancer, Scorpio, Pisces |
| Gooseberry | 2 | Taurus, Cancer, Virgo, Scorpio, Pisces |
| Grapes | 2 or 3 | Cancer, Scorpio, Pisces |
| Herbs | 1 or 2 | Virgo, Scorpio |
| Horseradish | 1 or 2 | Cancer, Scorpio, Pisces |

| Plant | Phase | Sign |
|---|---|---|
| Houseplants | 1 | Cancer, Libra, Scorpio, Pisces |
| Kohlrabi | 1 or 2 | Virgo, Leo, Gemini |
| Lawns | 4 | Sagittarius |
| Leek | 2 or 3 | Taurus, Cancer, Libra, Scorpio, Pisces |
| Lettuce | 1 | Taurus, Cancer, Virgo, Pisces |
| Maple tree | 2 or 3 | Cancer, Scorpio, Pisces |
| Marrow | 1 or 2 | Cancer, Scorpio, Pisces |
| Melon | 1 or 2 | Cancer |
| Mushrooms | 1 or 2 | Taurus, Virgo, Libra |
| Nectarine tree | 2 or 3 | Cancer, Scorpio, Pisces |
| Nut tree | 2 or 3 | Sagittarius |
| Oak tree | 3 | Cancer, Libra, Scorpio, Pisces |
| Oats | 1 or 2 | Libra Scorpio, Sagittarius |
| Onion (seeds) | 2 | Taurus, Libra, Pisces |
| Onion (sets) | 3 or 4 | Cancer, Libra, Scorpio, Pisces |

| Plant | Phase | Sign |
| --- | --- | --- |
| Parsley | 1 | Taurus, Cancer, Scorpio, Pisces |
| Parsnips | 3 | Taurus, Virgo, Libra |
| Peach tree | 2 or 3 | Taurus, Virgo, Libra |
| Pear tree | 2 or 3 | Cancer, Libra, Scorpio, Pisces |
| Peas | 2 | Cancer, Scorpio, Pisces |
| Peppers | 2 | Taurus, Virgo, Libra |
| Plum tree | 2 or 3 | Taurus, Cancer, Scorpio, Capricorn |
| Potatoes | 3 | Taurus, Libra |
| Privet | 1 or 2 | Cancer, Libra, Scorpio, Pisces |
| Pumpkin | 2 | Capricorn |
| Quince | 1 or 2 | Taurus, Libra, Capricorn, Pisces |
| Radish | 3 | Cancer, Scorpio, Pisces |
| Raspberry | 2 | Cancer, Pisces |
| Rhubarb | 3 | Cancer, Scorpio, Pisces |
| Sage | 3 | Cancer, Scorpio, Pisces |

| Plant | Phase | Sign |
|---|---|---|
| Saffron | 1 or 2 | Cancer, Scorpio, Pisces |
| Sage | 3 | Cancer, Scorpio, Pisces |
| Salsify | 1 or 2 | Scorpio, Sagittarius |
| Shallots | 2 | Cancer, Scorpio, Pisces |
| Spinach | 1 | Cancer, Scorpio, Pisces |
| Strawberry | 3 | Taurus |
| String beans | 1 or 2 | Cancer, Scorpio, Pisces |
| Sweetcorn | 1 | Cancer, Virgo Pisces |
| Sweet peas | 1 or 2 | Cancer, Scorpio, Capricorn, Pisces |
| Tomatoes | 2 | Taurus, Capricorn |
| Trees (shade) | 3 | Taurus, Libra |
| Trees (ornamental) | 2 | Cancer, Libra, Scorpio, Pisces |
| Tubers (for seed) | 3 | Taurus, Cancer, Libra, Scorpio, Pisces |
| Turnips | 3 | Taurus, Cancer, Libra, Scorpio, Pisces |
| Swede | 3 | Gemini, Virgo |

| Plant | Phase | Sign |
| --- | --- | --- |
| Valerian | 1 or 2 | Cancer, Scorpio, Pisces |
| Watercress | 1 | Cancer, Libra, Scorpio, Pisces |
| Watermelon | 1 or 2 | Cancer, Libra, Scorpio, Pisces |
| Wheat | 1 or 2 | Cancer, Libra, Scorpio, Pisces |

**Flowers**

The general consensus of astrological opinion is to plant most flowers for an abundant display as the Moon passes through Cancer, Virgo or Pisces. Sow or plant out flowers noted for their beauty when the Moon is in Libra; for hardiness as she transits Taurus but for a reliable, sturdy plant one should wait until the Moon is in Scorpio.

Flowering annuals flourish best if planted out in the first or second quarter in Libra.

Most biennials, perennials and bulb plants should be started during the decrease of the Moon.

| Flower | Phase | Sign |
| --- | --- | --- |
| Aster | 1 or 2 | Virgo, Libra |
| Biennials | 3 or 4 | Cancer, Virgo, Libra, Pisces |
| Carnation | 1 or 2 | Cancer, Libra, Pisces |
| Chrysanthemum | 1 or 2 | Virgo |

| Flower | Phase | Sign |
| --- | --- | --- |
| Carnation | 1 or 2 | Cancer, Libra, Pisces |
| Crocus | 1 or 2 | Virgo |
| Clematis | 1 | Libra |
| Daffodil | 1 or 2 | Virgo, Libra |
| Dahlia | 1 or 2 | Virgo, Libra |
| Flowering dogwood | 3 | Cancer, Scorpio, Pisces |
| Gladiola | 1 or 2 | Virgo, Libra |
| Grass | 1 or 2 | Virgo, Taurus, Libra, Cancer |
| Honeysuckle | 1 or 2 | Virgo, Libra |
| Hop vine | 1 or 2 | Scorpio, Libra |
| Heathers | 1 or 2 | Libra, Scorpio |
| Hyacinth | 3 | Cancer, Scorpio, Pisces |
| Iris | 1 or 2 | Cancer, Virgo |
| Ivy | 1 or 2 | Virgo |
| Jasmine | 1 or 2 | Cancer, Scorpio, Pisces |
| Lily | 1 or 2 | Cancer, Scorpio, Pisces |
| Morning Glory | 1 or 2 | Cancer, Virgo, Scorpio, Pisces |
| Pansy | 1 or 2 | Cancer, Scorpio, Pisces |
| Peony | 1 or 2 | Virgo |

| Flower | Phase | Sign |
|---|---|---|
| Petunia | 1 or 2 | Virgo, Libra |
| Pinks | 1 or 2 | Cancer, Virgo, Pisces |
| Poppy | 1 or 2 | Virgo |
| Rock garden | 1 or 2 | Libra, Scorpio |
| Rose | 1 or 2 | Cancer, Virgo |
| Sunflower | 3 or 4 | Libra |
| Sweet Pea | 2 | Cancer, Scorpio, Pisces |
| Evergreen trees | 2 or 3 | Taurus, Libra |
| Tulip | 1 or 2 | Virgo, Libra |
| Vine plants | 2 or 4 | Virgo, Scorpio, Pisces |
| Wisteria | 1 or 2 | Cancer, Libra, Scorpio, Pisces |

Strictly speaking, there are no such things as house plants in a real sense, but in general whatever you do plant to keep indoors should be planted in the first or second quarter when the Moon is in Taurus, Cancer, Libra, Scorpio or Pisces.

If you do not like indoor plants, you might like to consider having at least one pot of aloe vera available because of its remarkable healing properties in the event of burns, minor cuts or insect bites.

**Herbs and astrology**

Herbs have a wide variety of uses and many, many Moons

ago they were the main source and general basis of society's medical pharmacopoeia. Today, herbs are now widely used by people in their cooking because they enhance an enormous variety of recipes, especially with the advent of the many different foreign cooking systems that have been introduced into this country in the past few years.

The best time for any herb is when it is reasonably young. All of these plants lose some of their efficacy as they grow older. Young plants tend to release their energies more easily than the older ones. It is one reason why the spring period is the better time for harvesting herbs in general although many may still have young shoots later in the year.

Despite the astrological advice given later, the best time to pick or dig up the herb of your choice is late in the evening, during the night or very early in the morning. Herbs that are gathered for their flower use ought to be picked during the day time hours. Those you harvest for fruit or their seed are best taken during the night time hours.

Many herbs, like lavender for example, are used because of their delicate fragrance but of course, quite a few herbs are still employed for their inherent medicinal values. Herbs tend to be grown for their flowers, leaves or seeds and most astrologers agree that, depending on which part of the plant you intend to use, the following guidelines should be observed.

If it is to use the flowers or the leaves then plant in the first quarter under Cancer, Libra, Virgo or Pisces. To ensure a sturdy plant Scorpio may be considered. For the best seeds it is best to plant in the second quarter while the Moon is in Capricorn.

When picking or harvesting any herb, remember that while the Moon is increasing to full, the plant retains a better and more fluid supply of its natural juices and essential oils.

With this in mind always harvest herbs while the Moon is in one of the dry signs: Aries, Gemini, Leo, Sagittarius or Aquarius preferably in the first or second quarter.

The following herbs are associated with the astrological signs as indicated.

| Sign | Herbs |
| --- | --- |
| Aries | Cowslip, garlic, hops, mustard, rosemary, carnation, chervil, basil, nettle, catmint, wormwood, geranium and cypress pine |
| Taurus | Coltsfoot, lovage, mints, primrose, mint, thyme, violet, marshmallow, catnip, rose, carnation, saffron, honeysuckle, jasmine, tansy, wormwood, yarrow and soapwort |
| Gemini | Caraway, dill, lavender, parsley, vervain, mint, parsley, anise, marjoram, liquorice, fennel, honeysuckle, horehound and oregano |
| Cancer | Agrimony, balm, daisies, hyssop, jasmine, parsley, sage, aloe, evening primrose, myrtle, cinnamon, lemon balm, hyacinth, bay leaves and water lily |
| Leo | Bay, borage, chamomile, marigold, poppy, rue, dill, lemon balm, tarragon, chamomile, clove, sandalwood, frankincense, camphor, eyebright and sunflower |
| Virgo | Fennel, savory, southernwood, valerian, chervil, dill, caraway, mint, morning glory, lily, horehound, lavender and marjoram |

| Sign | Herbs |
| --- | --- |
| Libra | Pennyroyal, primrose, violets, yarrow, catnip, thyme, elderberry, iris, lilies, ivy, St John's wart, lemon balm and bergamot |
| Scorpio | Basil, tarragon, wormwood, catmint, basil, sage, catnip, honeysuckle, nettle, onion, coriander, garlic and elder |
| Sagittarius | Feverfew, house leek, mallow, chervil, saffron, sage, basil, sage, borage, nutmeg and clove |
| Capricorn | Comfrey, sorrel, Solomon's seal, dill, tarragon, caraway, rosemary, chamomile, lambs ears and marjoram |
| Aquarius | Elderberry, fumitory, mullein, daffodil, sage, comfrey, rosemary, valerian, fennel and mint |
| Pisces | Lungwort, meadowsweet, rosehip, sage, lemon balm, basil, lilac, nutmeg, borage, lilies and clove |

# Lunar Gardening Lore

This chapter has been designed to help you to understand the general principles of gardening by and through the age and position of the Moon using ancient and modern astrological lore. Please note the expression "general principles". None of this is set in tablets of stone, because just occasionally, astrologers, like gardeners, will disagree with this "rule" or that piece of gardening lore.

In a few cases some astrologers might tend to take into account the positions of the planets as well but for our purposes the positions of the planets along with their mutual aspects are not taken into account here unless otherwise stated.

It is impossible to refer to "normal" or everyday gardening procedures because of the lack of space. If, when the reader is referred to the wide variety of gardening manuals currently available there will be a few anomalies that most people will take in their stride as a matter of course.

The general make-up of this lunar gardening guide is centuries old in parts, fairly new in others and relatively modern elsewhere because of so many and varied recent experiments that have been conducted by both gardeners and astrologers worldwide.

Over the past forty years or more I have collected and studied as much of the available material that I could and this data has been incorporated into each of the monthly recommendations that I wrote and that were formerly published by *Prediction* magazine for nearly fourteen years between 1990 and 2004 and again during 2011 and 2012.

## The age of the Moon

Each month the new Moon increases, grows or waxes in light to the full Moon. It then wanes or decreases back to the next new Moon. Halfway between these two major points are the first quarter and the last quarter that are the mean positions or stages between the new and the full Moons.

The secret of successful gardening is to know astrologically when to plant or sow different fruits and vegetables, flowers, bushes, shrubs, trees or herbs to maximise best results. Also, when there is no favourable time for such activities there are hordes of other jobs and tasks both amateur and professional gardeners may involve themselves with such as creating new fences and painting them, digging new ponds, attending to rock gardens, creating pathways, changing patches and beds for this or that and so on ad nauseam.

## The first quarter

As the Moon waxes from new to when it is about half full is the best time for gardeners to plant crops that produce their results outside of the plant like asparagus, broccoli, Brussels sprouts, cabbage and cauliflower, or celery – there is a long list. Grain and cereal plants may be included here.

There is always an exception to the rule; in this case, the

cucumber whose seeds are inside the fruit but for some reason seems to flourish best if sown at this time.

## The second quarter

Here, the Moon is increasing in light to the full. Annuals that produce their yield above the ground do best when started now. Vines do well as do the pulses, beans, peas, onions and peppers. Cereals and grains and tomatoes flourish especially in this period. If you are unable to work in your garden during the first quarter or perhaps are waiting for the Moon to transit a more suitable astrological sign the second quarter can often be as equally productive.

## The third quarter

This is when the Moon begins to wane to about halfway to its next new phase. Bulb and root plants yield excellent crops when started now. Biennials and perennials flourish beautifully as do most trees, bushes and shrubs. Quite a few berry plants, grapes, potatoes, onion sets and rhubarb do equally as well. Carrots, parsnips radishes and turnips yield excellent results when started during this period.

## The fourth quarter

Sometimes called the dark of the Moon because she is waning in strength and is now dying with little strength or influence until the next new Moon. This period is best given over to the more mundane garden exercises so use the time to dig new patches, turn and cultivate the soil generally.

Weed, edge paths, clear lawns and guttering. Clean drains, destroy pests and get rid of rubbish by burning or taking it to the dump. Always keep the ash and remains of any bonfire – it helps promote growth when mulched in with other materials and it makes a splendid base for a compost heap.

## Gardening with the Moon

Recognising these quarters, or phases, is just one part of the battle, for you have now to learn what to do as Moon passes through each of the astrological signs — a very important point!

When you have learned how to coordinate the Moon's age along with the sign she occupies at the times given in the ephemeris, you will begin to experience quite definite improvements in your garden.

The times given in the monthly listings are the moment the Moon enters each sign.

Unless otherwise stated, it is advisable to wait a little while to allow the full strength of that new influence to get under way. Allow at least half an hour to an hour for any place and time differential to take effect in most areas.

| Sign | Activity |
| --- | --- |
| Moon in Aries | Because this is one of the fire signs, logic determines this as a good period to have a bonfire to be rid of unwanted growths especially material that should be destroyed because it may be noxious or dangerous. Use the time to clean tools or electrical or mechanical machines. Also, cultivate, till and turn over soil. |
| Moon in Taurus | One of the earth signs, so it is most productive. Almost anything may be planted or sown but in particular, beans, cabbage, garlic, onion sets, parsnips, potatoes, radishes and turnips. Flowers noted for their hardiness should be started now for Taurus is a hardy sign. This sign also seems to favour fertiliser — apply as when necessary. |
| Moon in Gemini | This is the first of the air signs and it does not really favour planting or sowing. Destroy unwanted growths, weeds and pests. Turn soil and prepare areas for planting and sowing later. This is a dry sign and that makes it ideal for picking or generally harvesting crops especially in the last two quarters. |

| Sign | Activity |
|------|----------|
| Moon in Cancer | The first of the water signs, this is quite fruitful and ideal for watering, budding and grafting. You may also plant or sow out apple trees, asparagus, beetroot, Brussels sprouts, cabbage, carrots, cauliflower, endive, parsley, sage and spinach. Any flowers planted now will grow in abundance. Never cut wood when the Moon is in any of the water signs. |
| Moon in Leo | Of all the signs, this is the most barren. Start nothing in this period at all. Once again, use the time for turning soil, cleaning up, repairing electrical or mechanical tools or destroy pests and unwanted growths. It is safe to pick vegetables and fruit most now and lawns may be mown now to help ease their growth. |
| Moon in Virgo | In this moist but rather barren sign, quite a few gardeners plant their early spring flowers like crocuses, daffodils and snowdrops. Very often, flowers noted for their abundant growth do well when started now. Chemical killers for unwanted growths also seem to be more efficacious. It is not a good time for transplanting flowers, fruit or vegetables either. |

| Sign | Activity |
|---|---|
| Moon in Libra | This is perhaps one of the most useful periods for many activities. Flowers noted for their beauty and their fragrance flourish well and sunflowers always seem to grow with a sturdy stem. Plant beans, barley, beetroots and carrots — anything that has a root growth. Vines do well and seed for hay is most productive. Marrows, melons and peas should also yield excellent results. |
| Moon in Scorpio | Once again, this has proved to be a most productive sign especially for bulb and gourd plants. Peppers, strawberries, tomatoes and all vine growths will produce extremely healthy results if properly looked after. Grafting and pruning exercises are best carried out while the Moon is in this sign and is the best time for creating a new compost heap. |

| Sign | Activity |
|------|----------|
| Moon in Sagittarius | This barren and dry sign is often used mistakenly for harvesting fruit and vegetables and should not be. However, this is an excellent time for planting leeks, onion seeds and shallots. Leeks may always be left in the ground for longer than most while shallots are known to multiply like crazy once you have started them. |
| Moon in Capricorn | This is not quite as fruitful as Taurus, despite being an earth sign, but potatoes, radishes and even tomatoes seem to do extremely well if started now. The Moon passing through here will also help to encourage the handling and training of most animals. After grafting or if cutting back wood-stemmed plants, healing seems to be especially helped. |

| Sign | Activity |
| --- | --- |
| Moon in Aquarius | This last air sign is very barren and extremely dry and should never be used for planting or starting anything. This is a good time to catch up on cleaning debris and cleaning drains and guttering. Turn soil or prepare new areas for receiving new planting but do not actually do anything. However, harvesting and storing fruits are particularly recommended. |
| Moon in Pisces | As expected, this last water sign is extremely helpful and especially encourages all root growth. One rule of thumb used by a many astro-gardeners is that if they are unsure about when to start anything this is the sign that will usually provide a good result. Start celery, plant chicory and rhubarb. If unsure about which flowers to prepare, please note that most started from seed in this period tend to flourish. |

Those who want to include flower, leaf, fruit and root days in with this information are welcome to do so. However, if you find that this data seems to complicate issues then ignore it and be guided by the information given in the relevant chapter for each month.

# Void-of-Course Moon

It is a purely astrological point of view that one should never start or try to finish anything when the Moon is in a void-of-course phase. For centuries, astrologers have advocated this almost as a rule rather than anything else.

It takes the Moon about 28 days or so to circle the earth, and during this time she passes through her four major phases while she transits (passes through) each sign of the zodiac. The period between the last recognised, accepted or traditional aspect the Moon makes with another planet and the time it enters the next zodiac sign is called "void-of-course" by astrologers.

For centuries, it's been maintained that this is a time fraught with problems and, depending on the sign involved, almost anything is liable to happen. During this period, the Moon has nothing to influence its course, no direction or set path.

Such times may last for only a few minutes or for as much as a day or even slightly over. However long it is or whenever it occurs may be summed up as a short silly season that, although it may happen regularly, it rarely lasts for long.

The following is as simple an explanation of a void-of-course Moon that I can give for the reader to understand without becoming swamped in astrological technicalities.

When we arrange to meet or agree to contact someone for business or pleasure, we would probably agree to a time and place to our mutual satisfaction by saying we will do so. This is something we assume and take for granted more or less every day. We rarely question an action so basic that we hardly ever notice.

However, when things go wrong we do remember and often blame just about everyone and everything except ourselves. Perhaps what we should have done is looked at the Moon to see what position and condition she was in when we first made the arrangement. In addition and, perhaps much more to the point, we should also have checked where she would be when we agreed to our meeting.

You see, when the Moon is apparently not doing anything we don't seem to either. Human affairs seem to go a tad awry without valid cause and nothing really gets going properly again until the Moon enters the next sign and life takes on a more coherent shape again.

Without an ephemeris, that is, the tables of the position of the Moon and planets, you will not be aware of this. But with them you can take advantage of these periods and change your luck. These guidelines will help you to plan matters a little better.

Almost every other day the Moon can be void-of-course for at least a few minutes but on some occasions the period can last for up to a day or even slightly more but rarely for more than about 28 hours or so.

As we are concerned with gardening, these situations could affect or upset any work you might want to do or actually do in the garden. The reader is invited to experiment with what is written here. Within the chapters on the individual months you will find that the more serious or longer periods have been listed for when the Moon is in this position.

As a rule, most void-of-course Moon periods not only do not last too long, they don't happen that frequently either.

| Position | Interpretation |
|---|---|
| Aries or the first house | You may feel physically out of sorts. You could be basically unable to understand or decipher basic instruction leaflets. Avoid interviews. Make trial runs if about to start regular new routines. Be careful with sharp tools of unfamiliar equipment. Try to avoid direct competition. Check all personal identification documentation is correct and valid for the purpose intended. You may not like the face you have to show the world. You will probably think of what you should have said or done after the event. Don't worry too much; it is doubtful if anyone else has noticed. |

| Position | Interpretation |
|---|---|
| Taurus or the second house | Ensure you have sufficient money, chequebook or credit cards with you. Where possible avoid entering into any long term financial commitments like hire-purchase, leasing, hiring vehicles or tools or arranging bank loans. Personal comfort may be upset in such a way that it is not possible to reset the status quo easily. This rarely has anything to do with your actual finances for most of us tend have periods of fluctuating poverty. Quite often people are known to buy extra food or other kinds of supplies that they may feel are in low availability at the time — just in case! Once the period is over the materials are used up in the normal way of things. |
| Gemini or the third house | It is easy to get lost, even in familiar surroundings, directions become hard to follow and people seem unable to give guidance, to you, that is. Others interfere just when you least need it and routine, especially where concentration is required, is disturbed. The boss wants you, partners need your help. Those whom you rely on turn in shoddy workmanship, Brothers and sisters or local people and events may become a source of frustration. There might be problems understanding others or other people have trouble following your drift. There may be minor private or public transport irritants — even the phone is likely to go on the blink. |

| Position | Interpretation |
| --- | --- |
| Cancer or the fourth house | Family relationships become upset, relatives prove uncooperative and there is a tendency to argue about private matters in public; embarrassing scenes can occur. Domestic routine falls apart. It is a poor time to begin a diet or start a no-smoking campaign. You may be unable to express your emotions properly; the wrong things are said at the wrong time. People cannot always finish what they start or while performing one task, a half-finished one elsewhere springs back to mind. Little things go wrong at home; fuses or light bulbs blow, and if you go out you might fret as to whether or not you left the oven or something else on. |
| Leo or the fifth house | Not the best time to have fun in the wrong places. It is better not to join in with the boss even if he is in a playful mood. Games go wrong and children have the knack of upsetting the grown-ups without really trying; serious matters can dissolve into silly situations that we all experience from time to time. Not the best of times to start anything new unless your hand is forced. Hearts and flowers situations turn you off and dates go awry. Married folk seem to rub each other up the wrong way; hobbies become boring and relaxation hard to achieve. As a last resort the TV set goes on the blink. |

| Position | Interpretation |
|---|---|
| Virgo or the sixth house | Details somehow just don't or won't marry up and have to be checked and re-checked. Nit-pickers have a field day; people cannot spell even the simplest of words. Computer programs crash, your appearance goes haywire at just the wrong moment and secrets tend to be aired inadvertently by indiscreet people who should know better. Not the best of times to try to repair anything either for that will only make matters even worse. The daily routine fails at the first hurdle; pets take a liking to the furniture and road-works start up right outside the window. Repair men turn up out of time and the clothes or dish washer packs up without notice. |
| Libra or the seventh house | Avoid arbitration or peace making roles; public functions fail to start on time or are cancelled at the last moment. People don't take things as seriously as they should, Practical jokers seem to come into their own but, whatever their intention things fall flat or may even cause an accident. Even the press can get it wrong by being more lurid or sensational than necessary. People in general bother you and close personal relationships are liable to run into almighty differences over the slightest thing. Personal habits tend to seem more public than usual — throat clearing, coughs or other habits seem to become more pronounced and infuriating. |

| Position | Interpretation |
|---|---|
| Scorpio or the eighth house | Joint financial problems occur. People conspire against others or among themselves. Foodstuffs may go off, even when stored in the fridge. Secret love affairs come to light, scandals are revealed. Sexual tension is probable. What you buy may not fit the bill. Dustbins don't get emptied on time. Paper boys deliver wrongly or not at all. Simple losses occur and the items are frequently never seen again. Some relationships might not be all that normal. Partner's habits may upset. Joint finances or tax returns could give cause for concern. Savings may not be up to the mark and the chances of investing but possibly losing money do not appeal at all. |
| Sagittarius or the ninth house | Impatient and restless and you tend to either over-reach yourself or you may over-overplay your hand. You feel you are in the right until shown you are quite clearly in the wrong. All travel matters whether over short distances or long-haul air flights somehow seem to conspire against you. You may go from A to B only to find your luggage has arrived at C. Anything (seemingly) straightforward develops snags and you become unable to think straight and solve the problem. In-laws can behave like the comedians claim and it isn't funny. Students seem unable to study properly or duck classes at the wrong time for the wrong reasons. |

| Position | Interpretation |
| --- | --- |
| Capricorn or the tenth house | Anything to do with work and or career matters can and probably will go wrong. Instructions are misunderstood or printed material is completely misinterpreted. Postpone precision work of any kind and defer all important decisions until a more propitious time. This is not the time to break or even bend the rules. If out and about and driving yourself stay within the speed limit of the area. Don't trust your inner intuition, stay with the facts — if you can get them. Don't go down one road only to change later. You may begin to wonder if you are in the right job and parents' side with the opposition. There is cause for considering a hermit's life. |
| Aquarius or the eleventh house | Social relationships don't go the way you originally planned and there will be difficulty making decisions or getting others to make them. Urgent matters get bogged down for all sorts of many reasons. Ideas abound, but little action is taken to implement them. At home or elsewhere, the central heating, gas or electric seems to take on a life of its own and computers especially will have a knack of doing exactly the opposite of what you want. People make promises but fail to honour them. You may consider re-directing your ambitions into another field of endeavour entirely but after due consideration you realise what you have is the best — for the time being anyway. |

| Position | Interpretation |
|----------|----------------|
| Pisces or the twelfth house | Domestic plumbing often goes wrong and the weather changes sufficiently enough to wreak havoc with any kind of outdoor activity — including drying your laundry. Indoors, the office system fails miserably. Files are not where they are supposed to be. Electrical equipment takes on a life of its own. In hospitals, the patients find restraint hard to contend with and an operating theatre takes on a new meaning altogether. Travel across water is not recommended. Surveyors find dry rot or the damp course is faulty. Should anyone tell you that you are not behaving logically something seems to snap. You might laugh about all this later but only if the damage has been resolved satisfactorily. |

# General Weather Expectations

A survey that ranged from around the turn of the previous century through to the 1950s showed that here in the UK we seemed to suffer five seasons and not the expected four that comprise of spring, summer, autumn and winter that we have normally come to expect.

When the author of this survey broke his findings down in order to classify them properly (from his point of view, of course), he maintained that we have an early spring followed by spring then an early summer more or less together. This was followed by high summer and our often moderate and fairly sedate autumn, which then merged into what he called early winter after which came late or proper winter.

As we have always said we have only four seasons much of what he discussed has just faded away. Most of our modern knowledge and weather lore has been handed down to us through the years starting with what the ancient Egyptians allegedly first discovered through their astrologer priests.

No matter to whom we assign any credit here in the UK, we enjoy a wide variety of conditions for such a small area. What we have done over the years is rely on what happened in more recent times so that, for instance, we speak rather glowingly of the best summer we ever had which was in 1976 or the worst winter which many maintain began in late December 1962 and lasted through to around early March 1963.

Indeed, the weather we experienced in the latter part of 2011, the winter of 2012 and the excess rainfall throughout almost the whole of that year in the UK has rather dented the averages to be expected in the next few years. And as I prepare this edition, the early weeks of 2013 have certainly caused a few headaches so far. As the Sun enters Aries on March 20 the weather forecasts are suggesting heavy snowfalls and rain in the north.

But this is dealing with the extremes rather than the averages, which are far more comfortable to experience. So, with this in mind we will start with what we can generally expect from each month in far more moderate and average terms. As a rule, the UK is divided into two areas, north and south and this will suffice for this survey.

| Month | Weather |
|-------|---------|
| January | Generally, this tends to be the coldest month of the year with temperatures that can range from below zero centigrade to around 2° to 8° centigrade, it being a tad colder the more north one goes. There are often high winds in the more open spaces in the northerly areas where we may experience at least 8 or 9 days gales and storms. The south of the country barely suffers such rigorous weather for the tendency here is to enjoy more sunshine. Rainfall ranges from about 7 or 10 centimetres in the south to 25 centimetres or so in the north. There is almost always snow on high ground. |
| February | No matter what sort of optimist you may be there is always a frost of some kind this month and temperatures range on average from about 4° to 9° centigrade. As a rule, it is a windier month in the north with a little more sunshine in the south of the country. The longer day is slowly beginning to be noticeable and rainfall is generally less this month — about 5 or 6 centimetres in the south with around double this amount the further north one travels. Snow persists but is much thicker in the north while the south often has none at all — but don't be fooled for it can be very heavy. |

| Month | Weather |
|-------|---------|
| March | By now the UK should be experiencing much warmer weather although there will still be frosts, and some of these can be quite severe. Daylight becomes obviously longer and the clocks go on at the end of the month. The rule is to advance the clock by one hour (spring forward) at 02.00 hours on the last Sunday night in the month. Cloud cover may last longer although we all tend to see more actual sunlight this month. Rainfall ranges from around 5 centimetres to 25 centimetres or so but low-lying areas become prone to flooding as snow on the high ground begins to melt. |
| April | Despite spring having arrived finally this month, one should still beware of sudden cold snaps and frosts, especially at night which can be most severe. The winds tend to calm down into stiff breezes but the temperature change between night and day is very noticeable. Generally, they seem to range from between 4° through to 12° centigrade. Sunshine throughout the whole area tends to last for much longer periods. April showers do exist and they can be frequent although they rarely seem to last for any real length of time. Snowfall is more or less over although the extreme north can have the odd flurry or even stronger spells. |

| Month | Weather |
|-------|---------|
| May | The nights can be fairly cold but the days are much warmer. There is still the danger of sudden frost, so look after any or all fruit plants for if they are in flower, just the one frost will undo all the good work. Quite often, this can be quite a windy period. Generally speaking, cloud cover is always apparent but may be restricted to the eastern side of the country. Rainfall eases back although there may still be a few very heavy moments. Temperatures can be as low as 7° to 9° overnight while during the day they can reach as high as 20° or 22°. Snowfall is rare. |
| June | Once June arrives, the summer isn't usually far behind. Fairly comfortable nights precede some fairly quiet warm days and it all becomes far more bearable as the month progresses. There is rarely a frost to worry about for the temperature may range from 12° centigrade at night through to around 24° during the daytime. On average, rainfall is rarely more than 10 to 12 centimetres anywhere. Wind can be a troublesome affair, especially on open ground or in built up areas between high sided constructions. It would be most unusual to experience frost or snow during June but I have known snow on midsummer's day — 24 June. |

| Month | Weather |
|-------|---------|
| July | If not the hottest month, it is certainly one of the warmest with temperatures reaching very high numbers — often as high as 27° centigrade or even more. Humidity can also be high, especially at night. This allows a gardener to slow down a little and pursue his or her tasks at a more leisurely pace. As a rule there is a risk of thunderstorms in the final week, more frequent in the south rather than the north. Curiously, any winds we experience tend to be stronger in the north. Often, it becomes a shade cooler as the month draws to a close. |
| August | This is often a hot, sultry month with light rainfall everywhere so you should be prepared to water the garden yourself. Temperatures can range from around 12° centigrade to very high numbers in all areas certainly in the middle few days of the month. August is noted for its long steady spells of sunshine with rainfall rarely more than 6 or 7 centimetres. However, in the closing two weeks or so there may be sudden thunderstorms mostly over the high ground and more toward the north of the country. Snow is most unlikely except on very high ground in the far north — if at all. |

| Month | Weather |
|---|---|
| September | While you may still enjoy a few more quite warm summer days, you will notice the way daylight time has begun to shorten and it will be a tad chillier at night. The winds will pick up and there may even be gales in some places. Rainfall in all areas will become noticeably more frequent and will range from anywhere between 7 to 19 centimetres or more. Temperatures will remain summery for the most part but the nights can fall to frost levels in some sheltered spots. Snow falls are rare this month but very high parts of the north might get a spattering. |
| October | As the temperature starts to fall you will observe autumn arrive as all the summer colours deepen and change. Night frosts are more than likely to precede still fairly warm daytime hours. However, the winds tend to pick up and blow the leaves off trees rather spoiling the marvellous colours of the period. Rainfall will increase everywhere and range from between 6 centimetres in the south to as high as 18 in the north. The clocks go back this month and the rule is to turn back the clock by one hour (fall back) at 02.00 hours on the last Sunday night in the month. |

| Month | Weather |
|-------|---------|
| November | Winter is now on us with frequent low cloud covering and temperatures that can drop quite dramatically in a few places especially at night. Stormy weather, gales even, may be expected in most parts. Nevertheless, the autumn warmth still manages to show itself on a few of the better days when we may expect anything from 2° to 12° depending on where you are. Rainfall also has a quite wide range from around 5 centimetres in the south to around 25 or so in the northern areas. In some places the rain may give way to snow although this is more likely in the northern areas. |
| December | Winter now begins to take a firmer grip in most places although we can experience some fairly nice but rather weak sunny days everywhere. Winds can be bitingly cold and a few gales are likely. Frosts can be heavy and with the ever shorter days many will yearn for the hazy, lazy days of summer. Temperatures usually range from below zero to about a measly 7° centigrade. Snowfall rarely lasts for very long in the south and we can expect the possibility of a white Christmas. The usual post-Christmas bad weather is likely in the last week of the year so wrap up warm if you go out. |

The foregoing paragraphs are, quite literally, the averages as compiled from the UK weather experiences over the last one hundred years or so. They are quite accurate and if or when you do heed them, you won't go far wrong when you pay attention to the needs of your garden through the year. And, of course, at this stage all gardeners, irrespective of their skills, are well aware of what they ought to do as the year progresses.

## Lunar weather lore and expectations

When we add astrological or lunar lore to gardening a whole new world opens up. Experience has shown that by adding the following information to what we already know in the purely practical sense all aspects of what people do in their garden or on their farm takes on a completely new perspective. The success rate of what is grown can double in many cases.

Readers must not worry about any of the astrological data referred to here, for later in the book everything has been taken into consideration. You will not need to learn any new techniques in the astrological sense for it has all been taken care of for you.

We now turn to what we may expect when each Moon phase begins. But before we do that we have to explain what we mean by the expression "Moon phase"; how to find them and why we say what to do at these times.

It has long been a tradition to refer to the Moon as "she" or "her", as in astrology she represents the feminine side of nature. The Moon is the fastest of the heavenly bodies and (she) takes about a month to pass through the individual signs at about one sign every other day on average. As a rule, she travels at slightly different speeds which vary from day to day, week to week and month to month.

The faster she moves the more perceptive people are likely to be and the more speedily things seem to get done. When she moves more slowly people generally tend to find it hard to understand anything new and the tasks seem to be achieved more slowly.

The Moon is said to rule the instinctual side of our nature, our moods or unconscious responses to our daily life. Old habits die hard. She reflects an influence or power rather than actually starts anything new of her own because (in astrology) she is said to show no light (or powers) of her own. Thus, for many, the Moon is all things to all men… and women, of course.

## Lunar phases

At the new Moon, also called the first quarter, she is conjunct, or in the same place as the Sun, and is at the start of her waxing phase. On average, if there is going to be any rain it will be between now and the full Moon. The sky tends to be somewhat clearer during daylight hours.

The first quarter begins when she is in a square aspect with the Sun, or halfway toward the full Moon when she will then be in opposition aspect to the Sun. Rain in this period tends to be heavy and can last for some time.

The full Moon occurs when she is in opposition to the Sun. Here she is at her strongest point and, for the most part, her energies and powers at are their highest. At this halfway point in her cycle there is usually more chance of rainfall during the daytime hours than at night.

The last quarter begins her waning phase and as she begins to weaken she is said to be disseminating her energy and strength. Any cloud and rain directly overhead is likely to pass fairly quickly and the sky remains reasonably clear.

At these major points of her cycle the weather conditions indicated are usually experienced and, in addition, and according to the time of the change, the following weather is possible.

A Moon phase change of any kind between 24.00 and 02.00 hours during the summer months often indicates fair weather. When the change occurs during the winter one may expect frosty conditions.

Should the change occur between 02.00 and 04.00 hours during the summer it will be cooler than usual and showers are likely. In the winter months this change suggests snow and possible stormy periods. The change that occurs between 04.00 and 06.00 hours in both the summer and the winter times often heralds rainy periods.

A change between 06.00 and 08.00 hours in the summer time presages a reasonable rainfall while during the winter months it implies heavy rain to mild stormy conditions.

A Moon phase that begins between 08.00 and 10.00 hours suggests a period of changeable weather — neither one thing nor the other. In the winter it can indicate a colder period with some rain or snow likely.

If the change starts between 10.00 and 12.00 hours, rainfall and or persistent showers are likely. In the winter time the weather will become colder and there may be a fairly strong windy period.

An early afternoon Moon phase change between 12.00 and 14.00 hours in the summer or the winter presages rainfall with local conditions deciding how much.

If the phase occurs between 14.00 and 16.00 hours in the summer the weather will become changeable. In the winter time the implication is for a milder period to take place.

A Moon phase change between 16.00 and 18.00 hours in both the summer and the winter time usually indicates fair weather for a few hours even if the skies are cloudy at the time.

Between 16.00 and 18.00 hours a Moon phase change in both the summer and the winter period suggests the weather will be variable.

Much the same occurs when the change happens between 18.00 and 22.00 hours in the summer but in the winter there may be a slight frost. .

This series ends with a change in the phase of the Moon between 22.00 and 24.00 hours. In the summer it suggests the current weather to continue as is. During the winter period the weather tends to become slightly milder, but at night there can be an extra bite to the frost.

## The planets

In astrology proper, the procedures to adopt and follow are far more complex and involve setting up a chart, map or horoscope for the time and place, but this a book for a gardener and not an astrologer. None of this has any real value here for we are more concerned with what we may tangibly note and use. However, having said that, it should be noted by amateur weather forecasters that each planet is associated with certain weather conditions.

| Planet | Weather influences |
|---|---|
| Mercury | The swiftest planet of them all, and also known as the Messenger of the Gods, Mercury has always been associated with the wind, its strength and direction. Often, it seems to be the cause of all manner of effects where winds of all kinds are concerned – from the faintest of breezes through to gales and storms. |

| Planet | Weather influences |
|--------|--------------------|
| Venus | The planet we tend to use when we look for possible rainfall and damp conditions generally. In cold weather she helps produce hail or snowstorms. She doesn't seem to have anything to do with temperature movement. |
| Mars | Has a lot of influence on temperature movement and is usually held responsible for the upper temperatures we experience. Such ups and downs may be with or without rainfall for it brings excessive dryness and even drought conditions. It can sometimes be responsible for stormy weather depending on the relationship it has with other planets in an astrological weather at the time. |
| Jupiter | Almost always brings fine and dry spells but is rarely the cause of the kind of dry heat Mars may bring. At certain times it can be held responsible for stormy weather but in general it favours the farmer and gardener well. |
| Saturn | In a weather chart, Saturn is most unhelpful as a rule. It lowers the temperature, brings cloud and rain and is responsible for the grey gloomy times. In the winter it brings cold wind, hail and snowfalls. When the air is still it may herald foggy periods. |

| Planet | Weather influences |
|--------|--------------------|
| Uranus | Influences sudden changes of any kind at any time anywhere. It will also lower temperatures and create wintry periods than can become quite stormy. When excessively aspected it helps to produce severe gales, tornadoes and minor hurricane type weather. |
| Neptune | As a planet on its own, it has little influence and is regarded as a "still" planet. However, when aspected and depending on where that aspect is from it can be responsible for freak conditions. At all other times it seems to bring light rain. In cold weather it may start a sudden thaw. |
| Pluto | Pluto will either produce cool reasonably even spells or when badly aspected it will bring violent and extreme weather. Storms or hurricanes are possible as are severe hot or cold periods. Once it has been activated, its influence can be rather severe. |

## The signs

Each of the Sun signs is associated with weather conditions, although there ought to be a planet in the sign and, in simple terms for the layman, it needs to be activated by an aspect from another planet. Once again, an astrologer has to raise a map for the event but this is beyond our remit for this book. Nevertheless, depending on which planets are involved for there may be more than two to assess and what the aspect (or aspects) may be we can determine the weather for the area and time period involved.

| Sign | Influences |
| --- | --- |
| Aries | This cardinal fire sign is very warm and rather dry and can sometimes be responsible for winds that can be very strong. |
| Taurus | This fixed earth sign is both cool and rather wet but, generally speaking, it tends to be the farmer's friend for it has a moderating and steady influence. |
| Gemini | This mutable air sign is rather cold and dry. Under a strong influence it keeps the clouds moving but temperatures may fluctuate. |
| Cancer | This cardinal water sign tends to be cool rather wet and, if the right influences abound downpours are likely – but they don't usually last very long. |
| Leo | This is a fixed fire and rather dry sign with a hot influence on weather. However, it maintains the same still influences for some time. In the winter it helps snow to melt. |
| Virgo | This mutable earth sign tends to be more of a cold and dry sign that creates high winds and can be the cause of blustery weather. |
| Libra | This is a cardinal air sign and is rather more of a cool sign than anything else that helps to keep good weather overhead but breezes can be strong at times. |
| Scorpio | This is a fixed water sign and, if we are to suffer extremes of weather this will be the most responsible area to check. It intensifies whatever may be influencing us at the time. |

| Sign | Influences |
|------|-----------|
| Sagittarius | An air mutable sign, it tends to bring us dry, pleasant summery spells. Usually a warming influence and if strong in the winter period it eases a cold spell and induces thaw conditions. |
| Capricorn | This is a cardinal earth sign and, if the aspects are right expect severe weather in the winter for this is a cold and oppressive sign. In summer months it brings excessive hot and or wet weather. |
| Aquarius | This fixed earth sign can make the weather quite changeable, that is, dry one minute, and damp the next. Warm or cold it may bring thunder and lightning with stormy periods likely. |
| Pisces | This last water sign is mutable and its overall nature is damp, cool and rather mild. We rarely have bad weather when this sign is strongly aspected. |

# Part Two

# January

When the weather is a little too rough to venture out, spend a little of your indoor time going through all your garden machinery and tools. Sort out what you can sharpen or service yourself and ship off all those you can't manage. Do any of these things need to be replaced or could you add one or two items to your collection? Only you can answer that.

Because of all sorts of likely weather conditions at this time of the year, it is almost impossible to know exactly where to start. If the opportunity presents itself I would suggest that it would be more than helpful if you could sweep over your lawn with a besom broom or, if you haven't got one, a reasonably stiff-bristled version will do. Dead grass, leaves or anything else for that matter can be quite damaging and worm casts are dreadful. However, their excretions do at least show to remind you that the gardener does have some help.

Once this has been done serve the lawn with a top-dressing of fine soil and work it well into the turf. Don't just let it lie there on the top of the grass for if it gets blown away it won't do the job you intended. Work it into the turf with a flat edge of a tool of some kind, a shovel or the back of a flat iron rake will do admirably.

It never hurts to run a brush or just a long piece of wood along hedges to give them a bit of shake-up. This will remove moisture, dead litter and whatever else may be lodged in them. Don't go mad, but a few minutes spent doing this will help to reap its own reward.

Good gardeners will want to get on with digging in and cultivating fresh patches. Now, although the ground may be hard because of the frost or even just the cold the wise gardener would have first covered the area with a large piece of old carpeting or something heavy or similar to ensure the ground underneath did not firm up too much because of the winter cold. In an unheated greenhouse all you need do is cover your plants with sheets of newspaper overnight. But remember to remove them during the daylight hours.

January is an excellent time for the gardener to plan out an herb garden. Not all people do this, but it should be remembered that because these plants have such a multitude of uses and purposes they are worth considering. Once your planning is completed and your plants are sown out they need very little maintenance, other than the usual tasks associated with all plants, of course.

As a rule it is wise to plant herbs in such a way that they will not be overly disturbed by wind and, if possible, so that they may also have a fair amount of sunlight. Almost all herbs thrive in sunlight — very few dislike the light and they will be individually mentioned each month when and where it is necessary to do so.

It is worth considering that if this should be your first foray in to growing herbs then once you have decided what you are going to grow and where you are going to put them you should order your seeds from an established or specialist herb nursery centre.

So, back to the garden; sooner or later a few bulbs will start to show where you have daffodils, hyacinths and tulips growing. Use a small fork, a hand one is ideal, and lightly prick over the ground but not too forcibly, just enough to get at a few hardy weeds and to give these growths a better chance by aerating the ground.

Give your greenhouse a good airing. Clean it through, water gently; change the soil where needed and look out for decaying bits and pieces which should be removed immediately.

Clean the glass or plastic, oil the door hinges and the windows. After this bulbs may be brought inside. Some cuttings may be taken like carnations and chrysanthemums along with a whole host of other possible root cuttings to suit.

Some gardeners will plant out a few small items this early in the year like small salad plants, for example. Other useful plantings may be made of mustard and cress, radishes and small lettuces which should be started off in frames. Elsewhere, plant potatoes and onions, a few carrots, leeks perhaps and french beans, mushrooms and endive.

Flowers should also take up your attention about now. Some replanting will be necessary and remember when you change the soil in your pots to make sure the replacement really is fresh — try not to use old soil that has been doing nothing for a few months. This might mean a visit to a local garden centre but, of course, this is where you can also stock up on new seeds and mull over a few new ideas.

Plant herbaceous perennial and a few sweet peas under cloches and have a look at the state of some of your fruit trees and bushes while you are at it. Check the grease bands where you have used them and where it looks as though fresh material should be applied because now is an excellent time. Prune and spray whatever looks as though it might benefit from such an exercise. Almost all fruit trees should be sprayed and vines will respond well to a gentle pruning touch here and there.

While looking at the fruits, if you should have any cuttings made in the autumn of last year like currants or gooseberries they might need to be firmed up because of the action of frost or even snow if you had some of that as well.

It might be a tad early but if you have young fruit bushes, or trees for that matter you would do well to take some action against the conduct of birds because for them food is at a premium this month and they will treat themselves to the young buds. There are many different ways of preventing this but the best idea that has always proved itself is to cover the smaller bushes and trees with fine netting. It does not have to be there for too long – eight to nine weeks at the most.

Should you have fresh, young newly planted raspberries and blackcurrants they need to be pruned well. Cut them back quite low to not less than 15 centimetres for the raspberries but a little less for the blackcurrants.

If we return to the greenhouse now and you have a chance for a good clean-up you should begin to heat the place to around to around 17° or 20° centigrade (around 62° to 68° Fahrenheit) in order to get some of your flower plantings under way. Flowers sown now like antirrhinums, gloxinias and begonias will all do well.

If you have the time, try to take a look at your pathways and their edges. Repair and renew where you can and, while you are at it, this would be an excellent time to re-turf and patch unsightly parts of your lawns.

Again, and because of your local bird and animal life, it would be a wise step to cover these exercises with a fine netting until you see the young shoots growing and your path patching has recovered. When anything looks different or fresh animal life will always investigate and that's how all your efforts can sometimes come to nothing.

The work listed here to be undertaken during January is far from complete and is meant as a general guide only. In the following paragraphs where it is suggested you try to time your efforts with the phase and position of the Moon is not complete either.

Because it isn't mentioned in either category does not mean you should not carry out such tasks.

Each month the Moon becomes void-of-course several times and is a position that can occur quite a few times although most of these periods are quite short. Some may last for a few minutes while one or two may be for a couple of hours or so. These periods may be taken as reasonably harmless. It is when the Moon is void–of-course for a much longer period we should be ready to avoid gardening.

## January 2014

The Moon is void-of-course for the whole of the morning of the 4th, all of the daylight hours of the 6th, all day on the 13th, all morning on the 16th, all day on the 18th, all morning on the 21st, all day on the 23rd and all the afternoon of the 25th.

The new Moon is in Capricorn on the 1st and enters Aquarius on the 2nd at 17.04 hours. Sweep the lawn, other grassy areas and the pathways, clear away accumulated debris such as dead leaves and worm casts. Weather permitting, dig over soil in proposed new growing areas but remember this is not a good time to start anything fresh.

On the 7th the Moon is in Aries and a good time to have a small bonfire of any unwanted growths you may have. A light top dressing of soil should be worked well into lawn and grassy areas. Run a piece of wood along your hedges shake-up them up a bit for this will help to move moisture, litter and other matter lodged therein. This will be very helpful when it comes to doing other things later on.

The Moon moves into Taurus on the 9th. A few gardeners may wish to plant out a few small salad plants like mustard and cress, radishes and small lettuces, preferably in frames. Elsewhere, and if conditions allow, put in a few potatoes and onions, some carrots perhaps. Ambitious people might also plant leeks, french beans, mushrooms and endive.

While the Moon is in Gemini from around noon on the 11th you might like to give the greenhouse an airing and clean through. Use water sparingly and change soil where needed. Clear away anything that has decayed and give the plastic or glass a clean. It will also help to oil all hinges. Once completed you may bring in bulbs and even take a few cuttings from carnations and chrysanthemums along with other root cuttings to suit.

On the 14th the Moon enters Cancer and this will give you a chance to plant and sow much needed fresh growths but, of course, you may want to effect some re-planting as well about now. Try to change soil where you can, especially with potted plants and do ensure the new soil is fresh. It is early, but a few herbaceous perennials and a few sweet peas may be put under cloches.

Grease bands on various trees ought to be checked so that where necessary they may be refreshed. Continue along these lines for the Moon will be heavily void-of-course for a couple of days. We will move on to the 19th when she enters Virgo in the early hours of the morning and becomes full before dawn.

You now have an ideal period to consider adding to or starting up an herb section. Not everybody thinks along these lines but it is worth remembering that many of these plants have so many uses and purposes. Such an area is easy to plan out and the plants you do decide upon are, once sown out, in need of little maintenance other than the usual needs of most plants. Plant them away from a windy or shaded area and where they may not be disturbed too much. Generally speaking, most herbs love the Sun and as so few dislike the light they will be referred to each month.

If this will be the first time you have ventured into this area, then once you have decided on what and where you are going to do order what you need from a reputable, well-established or specialist herb nursery centre.

At around midday on the 21st the Moon enters Libra. This will give you the chance to look at your fruit trees and bushes more closely. You will almost certainly need to prune and spray here and any vines you have will also respond well to such touches here and there.

If you should have taken any cuttings in the autumn of last year of fruits like currants or gooseberries they will need to be firmed up because of frost action or snow if you had that as well. You will also do well to take some kind of action against the damages that birds might begin to do here. Food is short for them at this time of the year and they tend to help themselves to any young buds on these trees.

There are several different actions you can take to counter this. By far and away the best move is to cover the small trees and bushes with fine netting. You needn't leave it there for too long — about eight to nine weeks should suffice.

Any fresh, young or newly planted blackcurrants or raspberries need to be pruned well. Cut back as low as 10-12 cm for the blackcurrants but around 15 cm for the raspberries. This work may be continued while the Moon moves on into Scorpio on the 23rd partly because the Moon is void-of-course for two of these days

The Moon enters Sagittarius on the 26th and you should turn your attention to onions. Prick over the surface of your chosen area and if possible, spread some wood ash over the bed. Sow out in the greenhouse for planting later. Seedlings started in December should be just right for this exercise.

After the Moon enters Aquarius on the 28th, sow a few tomato seedlings if the greenhouse is heated. Otherwise do this indoors. Sage and thyme may be put into your herb section in this last week. Already established clumps may be simply broken up as you want and planted as you see fit.

Once the Moon begins her sojourn into Aquarius on the 30th, clear away old Brussel sprout stalks, but do feel free to leave a few actual sprouts to grow shoots that you can employ quite usefully later in the year.

# February

❀

The weather ought to start to ease around now and on those occasions where you can get out it is time to prepare spring seed beds and other similar activities. Roses need to be planted this month, but not if there is any frost otherwise you will have to do so under glass or in the greenhouse. Also, sow lilies and other plants under glass.

All bulbs should be planted out in mild weather where possible and alpines should be looked at for they will need to be firmed up where they may have been loosened by frost. The same goes for any heather plants as well as your fruit bushes or trees that may have been planted out earlier.

A few pruning exercises around now won't hurt, especially by the pond if you have one. Concentrate on all rose and standard bushes, but leave tea roses until much later in the year. When you cut back, keep a look out for any damaged or dead growths. If unsure cut the shoot back to between 12-15 centimetres. This will ensure a good display later in the year.

While we are looking at flowers, please note that gladiola corms will flower well when they are allowed to sprout in the greenhouse. Lily bulbs, sweet peas and pinks along with some half-hardy annuals may also be looked at. If already established, take a few cuttings of alpine plants.

A few adventurous gardeners have filbert and cobnut bushes in their garden. At some time this month a few small red flowers will appear. Around the same period a few catkin-like growths will also appear. Now is the time to be very careful how you approach the task of pruning these plants. Make sure also you do away with any unsightly or wrongly growing branches.

The idea of the bush is for it to look like one, so you may have to cut more away than you might like in some places but it won't hurt. Now also is a good time to attend to walnut trees if you have them.

February is also a very good month in which to renew or start a small rock garden. Collect some eight or nine largish stones, more if you have the space. Lay them out where you want, ensure you have a good drainage run and always choose a sunny spot for this area, never in the shade or under trees for rock gardens thrive in the light. Put in place plenty of good fresh soil, peat and compost around them and plant out your alpines as you will. .

Good gardeners will go all out now to complete their digging and making trenches. Break down any rough ground because once this is out of the way you can concentrate more easily on getting new plants to grow. February is always a busy sowing and planting period whichever way you turn.

Weeding and clearing away unnecessary debris and rubbish is almost always a bind but it has to be done. As you are carrying out the work you will see where the early slugs and other pests are raiding the good stuff (to them that is) so then are you can lay out the necessary repellents and slug pellets where needed.

While you are performing these tasks you may see squirrels visiting to see what they can get. If you have bird feeders on poles you may have to remove them to where the squirrel cannot get at them. If you really want to upset them, pile as much grease as you can up and down the poles. After leaping on to them and sliding down a couple of times they soon give up and go elsewhere. The expression on their little faces is an absolute joy to behold.

You may well spend a lot of time in the greenhouse and, if so, you will be able to gauge when to aerate the place without allowing in too much cold. Watch out for a high winds coming through the open door or windows.

It doesn't hurt to keep water in here either for it will be a tad warmer than outside. Your plants will appreciate that touch. While working in the greenhouse do remember to pot out annuals that you may have sown in the late summer last year for flowering later this year. If you put them singly in 10–12 centimetre high pots then place them on the shelves for this will encourage them to become quite strong.

Early vegetables can now be safely sown under cloches. A small selection of a few broad beans will flourish preferably of you space them out at about 5-6 centimetres apart rather just throw the seed into the soil willy-nilly. In the greenhouse you may sow cauliflower, peas and lettuce. A few cucumbers sown now will reap out nicely later in the year.

Other vegetables that may be started during the month are parsnips which should be sown out at about 20–25 centimetres apart. Early beetroot started now will be ready for the middle of June. These don't require so much space as the seeds are larger by comparison than with most other vegetables. Early celery, a few shallots along with a selection of cabbage, broccoli and even a few early parsnips should do well.

For those who like them, Jerusalem artichokes can also be planted out about 30-35 centimetres apart. As these plants can grow to the height of a man they will create a certain amount of shade and act a wind-break when as they do come to maturity — useful if looking for a temporary shady area for other things.

Another sowing of main crop tomatoes planted out separately in very small pots — about 5 or 6 centimetres or so will suffice here. If it is reasonably warm there is no reason why a few early turnips can't be planted out in the garden. Only sow a few at a time to start with and place them about 25-30 centimetres or so apart. Once they are under way you may repeat this every three weeks or so until mid-summer. This method creates a series of fresh young plants as against the chance of some old tough ones possibly spoiling a meal.

Toward the end of the month, and when you have the time, hedges may be added to with young plants but preferably when it is mild and dry. Try to keep them fairly frost free for a short while until they root and settle in properly.

This is also a good time to trim back any overgrown parts of hedges and it wouldn't hurt to have another sweep of the lawn and then aerate it as best you can. The essential thing is to remove the worm casts as often as possible. Moss or weed growth should be treated now to minimise the problems they could bring later on.

The work listed here to be carried out during February is not complete by any means and has been compiled as a general guide only. The following paragraphs where it is suggested you try to time your efforts with the phase and position of the Moon is not complete either. Because it isn't mentioned in either category does not mean you should not carry out such tasks.

## February 2014

During February the Moon will be void-of-course all day on the 7th, 12th, 17th, the morning of the 24th, and from about 11.00 hours until 15.00 hours on the 26th and 28th.

As a last quarter Moon she enters Pisces on the 1st and then Aries on the 3rd. Much will depend on the weather and how much time you have but about now would be an ideal time to put in your first rock garden. Gather up some half dozen or more large stones, more if you have the space, and lay them out wherever you want. Should you already have a rock garden check it over as advised here

Make sure that you put in a good drainage system and try to choose a fairly sunny place for this venture. The shade or under trees is not a good idea because rock gardens flourish so much the better in direct sunlight You will need plenty of good fresh soil, peat and compost to put around them and then you can plant out your alpines as you will.

The Moon moves on into Taurus on the 5th and will be in her first quarter on the 6th. You may now begin to sow out early vegetables under cloches. Broad beans, cauliflower, peas and lettuce may also be put out under the same conditions. Adventurous souls may also like to sow a few cucumbers for the chances are they will flourish well and produce a goodly crop later in the year

You may also start parsnips that ought to be sown out about 20–25 centimetres apart and even beetroot started now should be ready for the middle of June. Incidentally, they don't require too much space as their seeds are rather large in comparison with a lot of other vegetables. Put out some early celery, a few shallots along with a selection of cabbage and even a handful of broccoli should do well.

The Moon enters Gemini late in the evening of the 7th. Try to complete as much of your digging and the creation of any trenches you will need. Break up any rough soil well because once you have done so you can concentrate more easily on getting your new plant life to flourish. Regrettably, February is always a busy sowing and planting period whichever way you turn.

Weeding and clearing away all the accumulated winter's debris and rubbish is a bit of a bind, but it has to be done. While you are at it you are likely to see where any early slugs and other pests are raiding the good stuff (to them that is) so you can lay out the necessary repellents and slug pellets where needed.

The Moon moves into Cancer on the 10th. Make a sowing of main crop tomatoes put separately in very small pots — about 5 centimetres or so will suffice. If the temperature is reasonably warm there is no reason why a few early turnips can't be planted out. Sow a few at a time to start with and place them about 25 centimetres or so apart. Once they are under way you should feel free to repeat this about every three or four weeks or so until mid-summer. Doing it this way helps to make many new and fresh young plants as against the chance of some old tough ones spoiling things later.

When the Moon pushes on into Leo on the 12th it signals time to look over the greenhouse. You can now assess when to aerate things without letting in too much cold. High winds that come through the open door or windows can do a lot of damage because of the cold they will bring with them.

A little water for the plants may be kept in your greenhouse because it will be warmer than outside and your plants will appreciate it. As you work in the greenhouse remember to pot out annuals that you probably sowed in the late summer of last year for flowering later this year. Now is the time put them singly into high pots, about 10-12 centimetres high and then put them on your shelving to encourage them to become quite strong as and when they grow.

The Moon enters Scorpio on the 20th and a rather careful look is now required as far as filbert and cobnut bushes are concerned. About now or in a short while there ought to appear some small red flowers followed by catkin-like growths. Be careful how you prune and do away with anything. The bush should look like one so do not cut away more than you have to. Treat any walnut trees you may have in the same way.

The Moon moves on into Sagittarius on the 22nd and you can transplant a few autumn sown onions but space them well, about some 15-20 centimetres apart in rows about 30-35 centimetres apart.

A few shallots along with some garlic put in now won't hurt either. If you have any divide and replant chives. Lettuce and radishes may also be sown if the weather allows it otherwise put them under cloches

The Moon pushes on into Capricorn on the 24th and in the green house you should repot ferns while fuchsia cuttings put in at this time should take root quite well. If the weather is really nice and warm it won't hurt to make some (very) early sowing of freesia and verbena

The Moon enters Aquarius on the 26th and will allow you time to have a clear up in all sorts of areas along with an opportunity to dig over a few new patches — weather permitting, of course. During any of these exercises you will almost certainly see a few squirrels paying their visits to see what the can get at. To keep them less interested in the bird feeder arrangement you have rub as much grease as you can up and down the poles. After a couple of false tries as they slide down again and again they will probably give up and go off and annoy other folk. And while digging keep an eye open for those alert little robins. They can be so friendly and will come up quite close as you dig and if you and they spot a worm or other life please stop to allow them to get down on the surface and enjoy their repast. As the year wears on they keep a lookout for you. The moment you appear so will they, so you can both enjoy your garden.

# March

☀

Much of the colder weather should have gone by now and we ought to be able to start to enjoy spring-like weather — hopefully. Although spring doesn't actually start until the Sun enters Aries, usually on the 21st, we should be able to get quite a few of our tasks under way long before then.

The days will now be noticeably longer and it is important that you ensure you maintain a steady greenhouse temperature all the time. Around 14° to about 18° centigrade should be the norm for a while. The soil may seem to be a little harder than usual and needs to be broken up, especially if you are going to rotate some of your more regular planting areas.

This is a good time to repot and replant growths like wall-flowers, forget-me-knots or double daisies. Break up clumps of some of your older perennials by dividing them into smaller pieces and replant using fresh soil. You will notice that succulents and cactus plants tend to drink a lot now and will need watering more frequently and so also will any plants you have brought indoors. Some authorities also claim that carnations seem to drink more frequently about now.

March is good for planting out trees, bushes and even hedge renewal can be safely undertaken — at the right times of course. As a rule a hedge, provided it is well placed (that is, if it is not primarily acting as a border between you and your neighbour), can often be quite useful as a windbreak for it provides a useful shelter for all kinds of flowering shrubs and other plants.

This in itself allows you to have a colourful area here instead of just plain green privet. March is just about the last time you can reasonably expect success from hedge planting. If you plant any later in the year the roots may not have sufficient time to become established.

Really serious attention should now be paid to all lawns as well for turf-laying which is often carried out during this period. As you work here and there you will almost certainly see where you can clear away all manner of unwanted bits and pieces. If you are laying turf or starting a whole new lawn this is the best time of the year to put everything into action. Borrow or hire a light roller to help press the new top into place.

All of your pathways will probably need some work on them and, if you have one you should look at the state of your drive as well especially if it is tarmac or of a similar type. Check all steps — even if it is only a one up. Now is the time to make everything usable and in good condition for people of all ages. If any annual weeds have returned then use your hoe although what you will have left may not look overly attractive it will soon look nice again.

The vegetable section of the garden becomes very important in March. There is very little that you can't plant or sow but, probably because of the size of your particular area in most cases, you have to be selective as you move around.

During March onion sets, that is, onions that have had their growth stopped toward the end of last year may be planted out as can more peas, carrots, cabbage, parsnips and sprouts. Leeks from seed may be started about now to allow you to plant out around mid-June.

While it may be a tad early in some areas, kohlrabi may be started from seed about now although April might be better if the weather is poor. If you have any it won't hurt to plant a few early asparagus plants either. With what you have already under way this rather widens the choice of vegetables enough for most folk.

For the salad lovers, lettuce, radish and even a few early cucumbers may be sown. Some folk have even started beetroot this month, although it is about a few weeks or so early. It isn't too late to divide and replant chives either for they are a good substitute for onions. You could even start a little chicory in the greenhouse for this can be eaten raw in a salad. Much depends on the weather for such things to become successful.

The flower garden begins to go quite mad about now and you do become so spoilt for choice. Of course you won't use half what may be suggested here but you will have a wide enough range to suit most tastes. The adventurous may even stop growing one in favour of something new for a change.

Hardy and half-hardy annuals are usually started this month and among them will almost certainly be clarkia and convolvulus. Alyssum will be a must for those who want make their rockeries a little more colourful. Lobelia is a firm favourite as is helianthus (preferably the small "dwarf sun-gold" variety), which does not grow to more than about 60 centimetres as a rule.

Gypsophila, nigella or "love-in-a-mist" and begonia all have lovely early displays and give the garden some colour while you are waiting for everything else to mature. The list is virtually endless.

We may not suffer from them much these days, but March winds can do a lot of damage that we don't always appreciate until we see for ourselves what has gone wrong. It is advisable to make a check of the ties you put in place earlier to secure plants to stakes and wires. Also, make sure your labels where you may have had to use them are still in position.

For those who have patios of any size, now is a good time to look through all the containers so that where you deem necessary, repot all plants that could do with it. As you have already selected the variety of containers needed for this area make sure that all the water drainage holes are clear to allow free flow before you load in the fresh new soil.

If you have made arrangements to start a small herb garden March is a good month in which to continue to work on the soil and, if you have one, use a proper seed drill for this exercise. Allow about 20 centimetres or so between plants — at least to begin with for it isn't always easy to know how your herbs will grow. You may begin the month with sorrel, chives, some chervil, parsley and marjoram. Sow the seeds about 2-3 centimetres deep; amounts will depend on whether you want them for table use only or to keep some back for later storage.

The work listed here for March is far from complete and has been compiled as a guide only. The following suggestions for when and what tasks to try to time your efforts with the phase and position of the Moon is not complete either. Because it isn't mentioned in either category does not mean you should not carry out such tasks.

## March 2014

The Moon becomes void-of-course on several times during this March and it would be wise to hold back on gardening activities on the morning of the 9th and the 14th, all day on the 21st and 23rd, the afternoon of the 25th and the afternoon of the 29th.

The Moon is new and in Pisces on the 1st. Most flowers started from seed about will flourish. Lift and or replant where you think it will help and plant out your herbaceous perennials if they are ready.

The Moon enters Aries on the 2nd. As they are so useful, try to keep a pair of secateurs on you when in your garden because simple pruning exercises never hurt. Cultivate soil where needed, remove all decayed, dead or dying growths and, if you have enough, start the first of many a bonfire in the coming weeks. Rake over and keep the dead ashes for later.

Once the Moon has moved into Taurus on the 4th, use the time to look over your vegetable patch or patches for this part of your garden takes on an added importance now. There is very little that you may or not plant or sow but you may have to be selective because of the size garden you have. Plant out a few more peas, carrots, cabbage, parsnips and sprouts. It is a little on the early side but kohlrabi may be started from seed about now although April is more favoured because the weather should be better.

The Moon enters Gemini on the 7th and you should now turn the soil and prepare areas for planting and sowing. The earth will be a little harder than later on and it needs to be well broken up, especially if you are going to rotate your planting areas. Daylight is now obviously longer and it is important that give the greenhouse a quick check over. Try to keep a steady temperature of around 16° centigrade if you can.

The Moon moves into Cancer in the early afternoon on the 9th. As a rule hardy and half-hardy annuals should be started around now. Try some alyssum in the rockery with its variety of colour and don't forget that convolvulus and clarkia are equally as colourful.

Helianthus and lobelia are among the favourites of most gardeners. There are so many to select from but we must mention nigella or "love-in-a-mist", gypsophila and begonia for their pretty display of bright colour.

The Moon begins her journey through Leo on the 12th, which suggests the opportunity to examine and work on all paths including the drive if you have one. Check any steps for now is a good time to make good any defects in time for people who may have trouble in negotiating them. If any weeds have grown over use a hoe on what may be present and it will soon look nice again.

One the Moon passes into Virgo on the 14th in the early part of the afternoon, use the time to sow broad beans and parsnips. Time permitting, prepare celery trenches and work in your compost ready for use later.

On the 17th after the Moon has entered Libra will be a fair time to plant out trees and bushes. It won't hurt to affect any serious hedge renewal either because first and foremost they act as a good border between you and the neighbours. Secondly, hedges make good windbreaks if they are heavy enough and they also give some shelter for flowering shrubs and other growths.

The Moon moves into Scorpio on the 19th which allows you to carry out pruning and grafting exercises where necessary. It is also a lovely time to create a new compost heap if you wish. If the greenhouse can be kept at a fairly reasonable overnight temperature now is a good time to sow freesia and verbena.

Once the Moon has moved into Sagittarius late in the afternoon of the 21st you may sow main crop leeks under cloches if you have any doubts on the weather. A few more shallots put in now will really flourish as well. During March onion sets, that is, onions that have had their growth curtailed earlier may also be planted out.

The Moon traverses Capricorn from the evening of the 23rd. It is worth noting that most plants tend to heal better after grafting, and cutting back any wood stemmed growths is particularly recommended at this time.

The Moon enters Aquarius next, rather late on the 25th. Not a good time for planting or sowing so use the time to clear away debris, clean gutters and drainpipes, sweep lawns with a hard broom and weed pathways.

March winds do a lot of damage that can be avoided with a few simple and careful activities. For example, make regular checks on the various plant ties created earlier to ensure plants remain attached to where they are supposed to be. At the same time check that labels are still in place as well.

Those of you with patios of any size should take the time to check them over and also to look at all the various containers so that repotting plants can be done if or where needed. Make sure you check out the water drainage holes are sufficiently clear to allow a free flow before topping up with fresh soil.

The Moon, now in her last quarter, moves into Pisces early on the 28th. Repot and replant plants such as double-daisies and forget-me-knots. It won't hurt to break up some of your much older perennials. Simply divide them up and replant with fresh soil and place them where you will just to effect a change for the better.

Succulents and cacti start to drink a lot now and need to be watered more frequently. While you are at it take the time to give a good once-over to any permanent (or temporary) house plants. Also, remember that carnations will need that extra attention because they too take on more water than is usual about now.

The clocks go on ("spring" forward) one hour on the 30th.

# April
☀

For as long as the weather permits it would be wise to spend a couple of days using your hoe to thoroughly destroy the weeds. Make sure the ground is fairly damp but not overly so, and then mulch through wherever it needs doing. Clean up lawns, repair little lumps and bumps and mow — more than once for you may feel it to be necessary because they can take it now that spring is finally here. Further, the more frequently you mow now the less time you will have to spend gathering up and disposing of the clippings. Nevertheless, keep an eye open for little touches of frost because it doesn't take much to kill off young plants.

Having said that, this can be a pretty wet period and you may be limited in the amount of time that you can spend out in the open. So, in the event of too much wet weather turn your attention to any indoor plants you may have. Now is the time to give them a thorough dusting and remove any dead leaves. If needs be change the soil where you think it might be helpful and, when you have completed all this, give them all a slight watering but nothing too heavy. It won't hurt to divide, layer or take a few cuttings of any of them because they are well protected and they can take it.

Once you have carried out all these tasks, allow them all a little indoor fertiliser.

Dependent on whether you have a patio, and if it is a covered area or not, now is the time to prepare troughs and boxes for new growths and sow a few hardy annual seed in the smaller pots. If your patio is a wooden structure and in need of a paint job April is an ideal time to start your renovation work. If your area is a stone or metal construction use a spray to clear away some of the marks you simply haven't had the time to clean up before.

Those of you who have raised beds rather than pots on their patio should extend their care to these items as well. Also, please make sure that the elderly and infirm can manage to get about the area freely. A useful tip if you are planning for this idea where you are is that it doesn't hurt to put your containers on wheels to assist free movement when you need to clean up.

Should you still need to work under cover, transfer your attentions to the greenhouse where you may have to spend quite a bit more time than originally expected. Ventilation must be looked at and the temperature level must be kept fairly even. This will be especially so if you experience hot days and cold nights.

The wind is another problem so be careful of leaving any side windows or doors open for too long. Also, you will now be aware that a few pests have arrived, mostly spiders and greenfly. When you do meet up with them dispose of them as instructed on any canned pest destroyer you may have purchased.

Once outside, all of your vegetable areas will need some love and care along with some extra plantings needed to keep up the supply. Although it will be the middle of June before you do anything properly think where you want to put your celery and then prepare the necessary trenches.

These should be at last 80-90 centimetres apart and about half that for single rows. Dig down about 35 to 40 centimetres, break up the base and mix in manure and well decayed refuse if you have any. Add a level of top soil and more manure until you have a soft layer about 10 centimetres deep in which to place the young plants later.

We turn now to what you might want to call successional sowings of vegetables to keep up a regular supply of all your garden goodies. More carrots, broad beans, peas, lettuces, potatoes, radishes and mustard and cress will all be helpful.

If you have the room plant out asparagus crowns, more broccoli and even early winter cabbage. Once you have planted all that you feel you can manage you must remember to keep these areas free from weeds and pests.

Earth-up where needed and don't be afraid to use a hoe where you can't get in by hand. Thin out parsnips sown earlier so that they will have enough room to develop properly — allow them about 20 centimetres apart within each row. If you have the time, you could set up your runner bean supports now. Initially, allow one seedling to a support held by loose string. If you tie too tight now the plant will be unable to expand or extend properly. You may use seedlings or sow direct as you think fit.

There is no reason why you cannot add to your herb garden this month. Plant out rooted cuttings of bay; sow some dill, fennel mint, hyssop rosemary and sage. Some extra parsley will not hurt either. Harden off under glass what you can manage from your last month's exercises in this field.

The flower garden will take up a fair amount of your time this month so it won't hurt to take cuttings from your herbaceous borders to use later. Delphiniums, phlox and lupins will all benefit from this. Finish planting out gladioli and attend to as many half-hardy annuals as you can. It won't hurt to plant out sweet peas, clematis, sweet Williams and foxgloves. If you have any you can now make up hanging baskets with whatever suitable plants you have available. Verbena, geraniums and trailing plants always look nice here.

In the fruit garden it is time to keep a watching brief on your flowering apple, pear, cherry and plum trees. Rather than spray them with anything now allow honey bees to do their thing and pollinate to their hearts content. But if you do spot problems then take the appropriate action accordingly. Your gooseberries and blackcurrants will certainly benefit with a spray. Where you can, remove as many flowers as possible from strawberry plants and, while you are at it spare a couple of minutes to look over your raspberries.

The work listed here for April is not complete by any means and is meant as a guide rather than as something written in tablets set in stone. The astrological advice referred to here should be taken in the same vein. While you ought to do this or do that according to the phase of the Moon and where she is at any one time this too should be read as a general guide because quite often it simply isn't possible to get everything done as stated. In these following paragraphs if something isn't mentioned in either category it does not mean you should not carry out such tasks.

## April 2014

This month the weather is so notoriously unreliable that one can never be too sure of what might happen mainly because April showers and a few hefty winds as well are rarely far away. To avoid any unnecessary waste of time you are advised to try to organise your time in equal amounts inside and out just to be on the safe side.

The Moon moves void-of-course on the following days and times so try to avoid working on the morning of the 3rd, the afternoon of the 5th, all day on the 10th, 15th and 17th, the afternoon of the 27th and the morning of the 28th. Avoid working from around 16.00 hours on the 30th.

The Moon is in her last quarter and enters Taurus on the 1st. Now, and while the Moon is in Gemini (from the 3rd at around midday) there are a number of small tasks that you will have to take care of as you mull through this month's activities. For as long as the weather permits it would be wise to spend a couple of days using your hoe to weed as thoroughly when and where as you can.

The ground needs to be fairly damp but not too much so. Mulch wherever it needs to be done and clean up lawns, repair the little lumps and bumps and mow — more than once if needs be. The more this is carried out then the less time will be needed to gather up and dispose of the clippings. Also, keep your weather eye open for any possible sudden frosts because it will kill off young plants.

This can be a rather damp time which will limit somewhat the time you can spend outdoors. In the event of too much wet weather now would be a good time to attend to any indoor plants you may have. At the very least they will need a thorough dusting. Remove any dead leaves, change the soil where it would obviously be helpful and then give them all a watering — but nothing too heavy.

It doesn't hurt about now to divide, layer or take any cuttings from any of them because being indoors they are well protected and can take it. Afterwards, give them all a little indoor fertiliser.

The Moon moves into Cancer during the evening of the 5th. You can now start what might be termed as the successional sowing of vegetables like broad beans, carrots, broad beans, lettuces potatoes, peas and mustard and cress will all be helpful. If time is available work on your asparagus crowns, plant more broccoli and even some early winter cabbage.

As the Moon moves into Leo on the 8th put cloches over strawberries which ought to help a few to ripen early. Spray gooseberries to prevent mildew and spray pears just before they flower. When the Moon moves into Libra on the 13th you should turn to the flowers in your garden for this will be a busy area throughout April.

Plant out gladioli and half-hardy annuals along with clematis, gladioli, sweet peas, sweet Williams and foxgloves. Time permitting try to make up a few hanging baskets with what suitable plants you may now have to use. Verbena, geraniums and trailing plants can help a lot here.

The Moon enters Scorpio on the 15th at 16.20 hours leaving little daylight for any further tasks you might want to carry out. It won't hurt to take any cuttings from any of the herbaceous borders and plants like delphiniums, phlox and lupins will all benefit from this action. After the Moon moves into Sagittarius on the 17th do keep an eye on the flowering apple, cherry, pear and plum trees.

Don't spray them yet, rather let the honey bees pollinate whatever they choose. However if there is anything for you to do then take the appropriate action as you see; for example you should spray your blackcurrants and gooseberries. And while you are at it, spare the time to take away as many flowers as you can from your raspberry and strawberry plants.

The Easter weekend starts with Good Friday on the 18th.

The Moon enters Capricorn on the 20th. Vegetables belonging to earth signs may be sown, main crop carrots, potatoes and radishes along with beetroot and swede seedlings. Dust with DDT where needed against flea beetle infestation. Get straw for the new (or refreshed) strawberry beds later. Thin parsnips and hoe between rows of earlier vegetables.

The Moon begins her way through Aquarius on the 22nd. Continue with these tasks as needed and set up runner bean supports. Allow one seedling per support to start and attach with loose string now. If you make it too tight the plant won't grow properly.

Once the Moon has entered Pisces on the 24th make the rounds once again of your fruit, flower and vegetable areas to attend to what is needed to at the time. Also, there is no reason why you cannot add what you might like to your herb garden. Rooted cuttings of bay; some dill, rosemary and sage, fennel and mint for example.

A little more parsley wouldn't hurt either. Harden off under glass what you can manage from your last month's exercises in this field.

The Moon moves into Aries on the 26th at 10.00 hours. If you have to spend any time under cover you could go to work in your greenhouse although if the weather has been that inclement it might be one of the last places you want to be in or near.

Good ventilation is essential at this time of the year and temperature levels should be kept as even as you can. Also, the wind might alter these balances so make sure side windows or doors are not left open for too long. Any plant life too near these entrances to outside can suffer so easily.

For the rest of the month that you have available (the Moon is void-of-course for two and a half days this week) would be well spent searching for any evidence that a few pests have arrived, mostly spiders and greenfly probably. If you do find any, clear them away with your pest removal purchases.

# May

❖

By now it is reasonably well into late spring or early summer, but you must still be on the alert for a few night frosts which can and do often occur out of the blue despite any (official or unofficial) weather forecasts. The best advice is to keep a few covers of whatever material you may have spare, even old newspapers will do the trick in most cases — just a precaution, you never know this month.

Initially, and this may seem unreasonable, do examine any or all new plants you buy or obtain, including nursery or shop bought sources. It is a wise gardener who will empty out his (or her) new plants from their containers, shake the plant well and then repot with their own fine, fresh new soil. When a plant is bought in this manner it is always possible that you may also have bought a few small white grubs which thrive on fresh young roots. This action determines they will get no further and you won't have to resort to spraying chemicals unnecessarily at a later date.

As the month progresses and it begins to warm up watering well becomes a necessary daily task; perhaps twice a day in some areas. Hanging baskets suffer the most as a rule because they will almost certainly be hung in an exposed spot bearing the brunt of the wind and sun.

Where possible try to use rain water from your barrels. Most plants don't like too much tap water but if that is all you have then be gentle as you spray. Try to spray the roots of a plant rather than the plant itself.

As you carry out these little tasks remember to water the roots of newly purchased shrubs and trees It only takes a few dry days with a little bit of wind and the soil simply dries up.

It does help if you mulch in a little manure or compost around the base for this helps retain water. However, water first and then spread whatever you want to use afterward. Try to water in the early hours, not too late in the evening and certainly not during the middle of the day.

This is the right time of the year to run your eyes over any ponds you may have in your garden whether they have fish in them or not. Duckweed and blanket weed will be heavy and you need to clear as much of this as you can. To offset this kind of growth have a few floating water lilies on the surface for when they begin to open their leaves later on in the year they will help to ease the problem.

Before you feed your fish, if you have any that is, drain the pond as much as you dare without harming them then refill it slowly until you have reached the desired levels. Although these creatures can and do tend to look after themselves try to feed them at least every other day but a little more often if they are active.

In among the flower beds now you should be prepared for signs of greenfly especially on your rose plants. This may entail the use of a spray where there is a serious infection. It doesn't hurt to check out plum trees for the same problem as greenfly tend to gather on these although they seem to prefer the younger or newer growths.

Slugs are another more serious problem for they love more or less all your younger plant life and they are terribly destructive creatures. Salt will be effective but is messy so use either proprietary powders or slug pellets.

Incidentally, where there are slugs there are often snails and they can be just as troublesome. If you pick them off plants by hand you can always leave them out in the open on a path — the birds will be down like a shot, especially parents with their young still in the nest.

If you thought you might have been busy in April then May will certainly be a challenge as you move through the rest of your other flower beds. There is so much to attend to. You should now be planting out seeds of hardy and half-hardy annuals. Pot on carnations, plant out chrysanthemums, dahlias and if you have any, other water plants. If you haven't already done so, you should now lift daffodil and tulip bulbs to create more space for your summer beddings plants.

Put down suitable catching material alongside your hedges and clip them where needed. Remove the clipping in the material and hold on to it. After this, hoe and weed as thoroughly as you can under the hedges. If you still have any heather left to plant out mulch the ground first with peat and some of the hedge clippings and top dress the older plants. If you have any problems with your alpines now is the time to weed with your hands or with a short hand held hoe if you have one.

It is time now to turn to the vegetable plots for there is a lot of preparation work to be carried out this month. You will need to create the areas you want to use for marrows so that you may sow the seeds but thin them out later. Prepare a site for more tomatoes and also for cucumbers and courgettes under cloches. Sow some more summer spinach, main crop peas, endive and kohlrabi if you wish.

You will also want to sow more lettuce, radishes, mustard and cress. It won't hurt to put in a few more turnip seeds either and, perhaps, some chicory and chard seeds would be helpful now. Also this month you may now plant out winter greens from earlier sowings, some celery and tomatoes.

Quite a few vegetable and flower plants can now be safely taken from the greenhouse or from under other sheltered places. This means you will have more room to start other exercises, perhaps not this month but at least you could have a good clean-up now that you have the space. Check under the greenhouse for small animal life and while you are at it, check under the garden shed. You will be surprised at what you might find. Mice love this space and don't be surprised if you find a rat hole either. Take the necessary action quickly.

Fruit bushes will have to be looked at during the month so when you have time remember to prune your raspberries, remove extra or unnecessary runners from strawberries and spread some straw under them to protect the fruit as it matures.

Once again, please remember that the tasks for this month referred to here are not a complete list by any means. It simply isn't possible to get everything done as might be hoped for there is so much to do and you may not have the time to get it all done. Also, the astrological advice that follows on now should be taken in much the same way. Keep to the days and times because that is important but it may not always be possible to carry out all these tasks where your personal time is concerned.

## May 2014

During this month there will be a slightly above average number of times when the Moon is void-of-course during daylight hours. These are all day on the 2nd, 5th, 10th, 11th, 12th, 16th, the morning of the 21st, all day on the 23rd, 27th, 29th and the morning of the 30th.

As May opens the Moon is in her last quarter in Gemini. Remember that frosts are still possible even this late in the year. Keep whatever spare material or even old newspapers just in case. Make a point of examining new plants from wherever you get them. Wise people empty their new plants from the containers and repot with fresh new soil. New plants bought often have small unwanted grubs that thrive on young roots. Cleaning off all the old soil will also rid you of any pests and you won't have to spray unnecessarily later.

The Moon moves into Cancer on the 3rd and as the month wears on it really starts to warm up. Watering is now almost a necessary daily task; perhaps twice a day in some places. Try not to forget your hanging baskets because apart from being forgotten at times they are also probably hung in exposed places where the wind and Sun bear down quite heavily at times. If you can, give them rain water from your barrels because quite a few plants dislike too much tap water but, if all you have is tap water at the time then spray gently. Spray the roots of the plants rather than the plant itself.

Try to water the roots of newly purchased shrubs and trees because it only wants a few dry days with a little bit of wind and the soil will dry up. It helps if you mulch in a little manure or compost around their roots for it will help the plants to retain the moisture a little longer. It is better to water in the early hours, perhaps not too late in the evening but certainly not in the middle of the day.

Run your eyes over your pond now because whether you have fish or not blanket weed or duckweed will lay heavy and you must clear this away. Water lilies on the surface can stop a lot of this type of unwanted growth. And before you feed the fish (if you have any) drain the pond right down but refill slowly until your levels are back again. While fish do look after themselves try feeding them every other day — a little more if they are active.

The Moon enters Leo late on the afternoon of the 5th. Clean electrical and cutting tools carefully and do check the wiring is in good shape. Look out for greenfly, especially on your roses. You may have to spray any serious infections. Do the same for plum trees.

Slugs are also a serious problem for they turn to the more succulent young plants life and can be very destructive. Salt is messy so use proprietary powders or slug pellets. Where you do find slugs pick them off by hand and leave them out in the open. The birds will be down like a shot – especially parents with their young.

The Moon starts to travel through Virgo on the 8th and flowers noted for their abundance may be put out. Stand bedding plants near or by a sheltered spot to help them harden off. Thin beetroot and carrot seedlings, Hoe well between the rows of onions and prepare the ground for planting outdoor tomatoes later in the month.

As the Moon moves into Libra mid-morning on the 10th flowers noted for their attractiveness should flourish as will those that have a singular fragrance associated with them. With the limited time you now have available work through the rest of your flower beds as far as you can. Put out seeds of hardy and half-hardy annuals, pot on carnations and plant out chrysanthemums and dahlias.

The Moon enters Scorpio on the 13th. If you haven't already lifted the old daffodil and tulip bulbs to give more space for your summer planting do so now. Hedges should be trimmed about now and, until you can dispose of it all properly put the clippings into suitable holding material. Hoe and weed as thoroughly as you can under the hedges and if you still have any heather to plant out mulch with peat and some of your fresh hedge clippings and top dress older plants.

As the Moon begins to traverse Sagittarius on the 15th you should look to the vegetable plots. You may have to prepare areas that you will want to use for marrows so that you may sow the seeds later. You can also start a plot for cucumbers and courgettes, but under cloches.

When the Moon passes through Capricorn on the 17th you should look at your fruit bushes and your raspberries for any pruning needed.

Cut away unnecessary runners from the strawberries and spread more straw underneath protect them as they mature.

Once the Moon enters Aquarius on the 19th check under greenhouses for there will be animal life you won't want. Also, look beneath the floor of the garden shed for you will be rather surprised at what you find here as well. In particular, mice love this area as do rats so take action quickly.

The Moon enters Pisces on the 21st at around midday and now it will be good to sow lettuce, radishes, mustard and cress, a few turnip seeds and, perhaps, some chicory and chard seeds. If you have the time and space plant out winter greens from earlier sowings.

As the Moon moves into Aries on the 23rd in the late afternoon you should begin clean-up exercises. Start by clearing gutters and down pipes, sweep the pathways, weed the edges of the lawns and make sure drains are clean.

Because of the void-of-course Moon times between now and the end of the month choose what actions you take with care. Tasks for May referred to here are not a complete list by any means and there is so much to do you may not have the time to complete it all. Try to keep to the astrological advice if you can.

# June

✿

As this month opens many people take it for granted that, unofficially at least, summer begins on the 1st of June each year. While that may be true, it is still going to be a busy period. In normal circumstances a gardener would have a few priorities in that this takes precedence over that or that this must be done before now and so on.

June is slightly different. Much of the gardener's time should be spent among the flower beds rather more than usual. Fruit trees and bushes will be high on the list while the food sections, although busy as usual, will need a trifle less attention.

Hardy herbaceous borders will need to be cut back and much work will have to be spent on the various types of roses you have. Cut away any small side shoots, hoe well between the plants and water well miniature roses. Hybrid and tea roses will shortly be coming into their own and making their rather striking appearance this month. They will need to be carefully disbudded in much the same way as usual. If you take away as many of the small buds as you can the remaining heads will enjoy a greater freedom.

Train the climbing and the rambler roses thoroughly otherwise they will go mad and simply overtake their part of the garden to the detriment of neighbouring growths. Remove all sucker shoots where you see them. Elsewhere, deadhead all other roses either if they have faded or, of course, are serving no more useful purpose. This can be done by hand most of the time otherwise use secateurs. This will allow the plant to conserve its energies into producing only the best.

Established lawns will need to be mowed regularly. If the weather is dry then spike the lawn first. Clean away all weeds, apply new seed and cover with a little piece of netting to keep the birds away. Lift as many remaining spring bulbs as you can and prepare them for storage. It won't hurt to lightly trim hedges because they may need it. However, when you have finished gather in the trimmings to keep for mulching. Hoe and weed as well as you can under all plants.

Usually, this can be a fairly dry period so it wouldn't hurt to clear all your plants out of the greenhouse to allow you back in with a hose and cleaners. It isn't a pleasant task but it does have to be done and you'll be surprised at just what has gathered that had not caught your eye before. Remember to allow for night time ventilation which will mean keeping an eye on the local weather forecast.

Pools and water plants should be looked at because if the weather is sultry or a tad too warm there will be signs of aphids and midges. Algae often grow a lot more about now and that will need to be removed. Lower the water level and replace gently with fresh water from a hose or a spray if fish are present.

Alpines and heathers shouldn't need a lot attention but they will have to be weeded in the usual way. Clip where the plant is obviously untidy or would benefit in a similar way to the way you worked your roses earlier. Heathers like a gentle spray when you water them and it is wiser to do this in the early evening hours where possible.

Many of you will have hanging baskets dotted about here and there and they will need a lot of attention in the dry weather. Hose the roots of these plants thoroughly and let the water really cover the surface of the soil. Pin back any over long trailers to improve their general appearance.

We turn now to the vegetable garden and the work needed here. It will be much the same as last month with certain exceptions. It is important to earth up all of your recently planted potatoes but not all at once.

Take it steady and start the work a little bit at a time. It would be helpful if you pursued this task on three or even four occasions to give the plants a chance.

Sow lettuce, turnips, endive, a few more peas, radishes and mustard and cress. Plant out winter cabbage, sprouts, kale, savoy and greens. It wouldn't hurt to start some more celery about now, a little more chicory, certainly a few swedes, marrows, and, if you think you can do it well, why not try a few leeks. Later in the month try your hand at some spinach beet using the method we described in April for beetroot.

Apart from mentioning an odd job here and there fruit hasn't exactly been at the top of the list. This month it will quite be the reverse for there is so much to get done. All fruit trees and bushes must be carefully checked over for any infestation and if any is found it must dealt with promptly and with the right materials.

All fruit is prone to something during June and strawberries are no exception. Look for grey mould and damage by birds, slugs and all pests in between. Limit runners to what you feel you can reasonably handle. Strawberries along with gooseberries may be thinned out or harvested accordingly. As a rule, I can usually selectively pick raspberries in the first week of June.

Apples and pears will need to be thinned out as will peaches and nectarines. Cherries, plums, damsons and currants will need to be thinned, watered well and, if necessary, added protection may be made by applying threads of ordinary cotton spread among the branches because it will stop the birds from invading the plants.

For those who decided to entertain herbs this year sow fresh dill, some chervil and put in a few cuttings of sage and rosemary. Pickings will be rich now so you can start to gather in either for a more or less immediate use or for freezing.

The leaves of rosemary, mint and sage may be gathered in as can sorrel, parsley, mint and fennel. Individual instructions for how each herb should be prepared for freezing ought to be found on the original packets that they came in.

In town gardens or on patios it is important that you water regularly — at least once a day if you can. If this is not possible it would be a good idea to top dress the plants with a little damp peat. Remove dead flower heads and, if needs be, you can always replace these growths with some of those from the garden

The work listed here for June is not everything that could or should be done but has been created more as a guide than anything else. In the following paragraphs you are given guidance as to when you should carry out these tasks in line with the phase and position of the Moon but even this is not complete either. Because it isn't mentioned in either category does not mean you should not attempt the tasks.

## June 2014

Once again there are several times when the Moon becomes void-of-course during the coming month. Try not to do anything too serious all day on the 1st, the afternoon of the 3rd and the morning of the 4th, all day up to 15.25 hours on the 11th, all day on the 13th and 15th, the morning of the 24th up to 11.05 hours and, finally, the afternoon of the 26th.

The Moon is in her last quarter in Cancer on the 1st and enters Leo on the 2nd. The first few days of this month are often dry.

It would be helpful to have a good clean through in the greenhouse. Take all your plants outside so that you can go back in with a hose. It may not be one of the best jobs in the garden but it needs to be done. You might well be surprised at what has occurred that had simply not caught your eye earlier. When you put everything back remember that night time temperatures and ventilation are important. Listen in to the local weather forecast, it could be very important.

The Moon moves into Virgo early on the afternoon of the 4th. Fruit trees and bushes should be carefully checked for infestation of any kind. Anything found should be dealt with immediately and with the right material as well. As a rule, most fruit falls prone to something in June and, for example, your strawberries will be no exception.

Look for mould and or damage by birds, slugs and all other pest life. Try to limit runners to what you know you can handle. Both gooseberries and strawberries should be thinned out or picked as you see fit. At about this time also look at your raspberries for there is often enough of them to help fill out a menu in these early summer days.

Thin out apples, pears, nectarines and peaches. Cherries, all the varieties of currants you may have, plums and damsons should be thinned out and watered well. It may help to add a little more protection about now. Use threads of ordinary cotton spread carefully in the branches because it will help to stop any invasion from your feathered friends.

The Moon moves on into Libra on the 7th. If we look around in the vegetable patches we will find what should be done and what actually needs doing. First of all, make the time to earth up recently planted potatoes but this will not need doing all at once. This is a task you may carry out on different days and when you have the time.

You may now plant out winter cabbage, some greens, savoy and kale. Sow lettuce, turnips, endive, peas, radishes and mustard and cress. Put in a little more celery, chicory, a few swedes, marrows, and, if you like them a few leeks. Later on, perhaps you might like to try some spinach beet using the April ideas we posted for ordinary beetroot.

After the Moon enters Capricorn on the 13th you should cut back your hardy herbaceous borders along with your roses. Any small shoots may be cut away and remember to hoe between the plants. A quick watering may also be necessary about now as well. To stop any invasion by your rambler roses into areas they should not go, train them all back thoroughly. Remove any sucker shoots if you spot any and deadhead other roses that are either faded or serving no more usefulness.

The Moon moves into Aquarius on the 15th and is in her second quarter. Spike the lawn well then give it a firm mowing. Remove any mossy patches and weeds, apply new seed and cover with netting to keep the birds off.

The Moon enters Pisces on the 17th and it wouldn't hurt about now to have a look at your ponds and pools. At this time of the year the heat is likely to encourage aphids and midges. All algae tends to grow faster and needs to be removed. Empty out about three quarters of the water and then refill slowly gently with fresh water from a hose especially if fish are present.

Once the Moon has moved on into Taurus on the 22nd you should take a look at your herb section and see what can be harvested about now. There ought to be quite a few items worth picking that you may take up for immediate use or for freezing. Pick off leaves of mint, sage and rosemary, fennel, mint and parsley. Instructions for how herbs should be frozen will be found on the packets they came in.

The Moon enters Gemini on the 17th. Grab a broom and other cleaning tools and wander around your domain clearing, destroying and removing everything and anything that shouldn't be there. Under hedges are favourite places to clean and make look presentable and once all your paths and other edges have been trimmed up the garden will be that extra bit attractive for both you and your visitors.

Once the Moon has moved on into Cancer on the 26th add to your herb area by sowing fresh dill, chervil and put in a few more cuttings of sage and rosemary. Alpines and heathers rarely take up a lot of your time but weeding will be needed in the usual way. Clip plants that are a tad untidy and give it all a gentle watering — especially the heathers that thoroughly enjoy a gentle spray, preferably in the early evening hours if you can.

Many people have hanging baskets dotted about here and there. They will probably all need a fair amount of attention in dry weather. Really water the roots of these plants as thoroughly as possible and allow water to cover the soil surface. Pin back long trailers to improve their appearance.

Whether you live in a town or the country, plants on patios need a regular and thorough watering at this time of the year. If anyone should be unable to do this it would be helpful for them to top dress the plants with damp peat for this will help keep the plant damp. However, remove and or dead head flowers here because you can always replace them.

# July
☀

Hopefully, this will be the best month of the year especially with those long hazy days of summer where we can all lounge out and enjoy the fruits of our labours — in more ways than one perhaps! Unfortunately, it does not always work that way. Extreme weather conditions can often occur during July. Rain can be quite heavy not only when the Moon is in the water signs but also even more so when she passes through the earth signs. The last week often holds this phenomenon.

You will be busy in the flower beds, among your fruit trees, bushes and other plants. All flowers will need your attention. Lilies will need to be dead headed but do remember to keep them to extract their seeds. Dig up and divide irises, trim chrysanthemums and ensure young dahlia plants are well tied up. Roses should be cut for their display and alpines will need to be continuously weeded and trimmed as will all hedges and other bush growths.

Water loss in your ponds is always a threat because of the heat so as you renew always do it slowly and gently. Lay the hose into the water and let the water run in slowly — the fish will prefer that. While you carry out this work you will probably have to thin out a few pond plants because they will be threatening other life as they mature and multiply. Do this by lifting the plant to the side but not out of the pond. This not only allows the plant to dry but also for any pond life to get back where it belongs.

Most gardeners tend to have watering holes of all kinds for the visiting wildlife. Do make sure bird baths and their drinking places are kept clean, full and fresh while also doing the same for landlocked creatures who come by either by day, like the squirrels or at night, like the foxes and, in special areas, the badgers. You may never know or see your guests at night but they do pass through. Sometimes they are most brazen while at other times you would never know what they get up to.

In the greenhouse many plants would do better to be in frames, pots or whatever rather than out in the open in there. The overly careful gardener may well have young grapes growing in their greenhouse and, if so, they will need very careful attention and thinning about now. The same goes for any heavy crop tomatoes that are grown in there. Ensure everything in the greenhouse is kept well watered but do it gently.

In your vegetable patches, you may be more inclined to harvest what you have already put out one way or another, but to keep up the momentum you will have to follow to ensure you have plenty. During July you will need to water everywhere most thoroughly but, as elsewhere in your garden this must be done in a more leisurely fashion for you can do a lot of damage with too much direct or hard watering with a hose that is locked on full.

As fast as you gather in artichokes, potatoes, onions, shallots, salad plants, runner beans, herbs and anything else you have chosen to be in your particular garden you will also have to plan out where your fresh vegetables will be planted or sown. Leeks should be put in this month as should spinach beet, swedes, turnips, winter cabbage and broccoli. Those larger types of radish may be sown out now along with a few more peas, potatoes, carrots and cauliflower to name but a few.

Find the time spend in your herb garden that you have been developing. When you gather in your herbs it is important to keep them apart — very few mix with other varieties. Pick only what you need. It won't hurt to plant out more chervil, dill and parsley in open ground.

Don't forget that lavender is counted as an herb and should be treated accordingly.

Fruit of all kinds should be harvested this month - apples, pears, cherries, gooseberries, currants and whatever else you personally have cultivated. After picking you need to thin or prune your trees and bushes which is almost a thankless task at this time of the year because there is so much to think of as well as keeping an eye on their overall healthy appearance. The slightest appearance of any infestation, bugs or similar must be dealt with efficiently and immediately or the rest could suffer.

If you have the time and because you will almost certainly appreciate a mushroom for they have a most unique taste you may find your present yield may not be quite up to expectation. You should now be looking to preparing a new mushroom bed. These edible fungi don't require too much attention but creating a first time patch does need a little effort and July is almost perfect for this exercise.

As usual, the tasks listed here for July are far from complete and has been compiled as a guide only. However, these astrologically based suggestions for when and what jobs with which you should try to time with the phase and position of the Moon are not complete either. Because it isn't mentioned in either category does not mean you should not carry out such tasks.

## July 2014

The Moon will be void-of-course three times this month and these dates are all day on the 1st, the afternoon of the 25th and the morning of the 26th.

As the month opens the waxing Moon is in Leo and enters Virgo the same day in the late evening hours. While she is here it would be a good time to layer your border carnations. Try to find the time to also plant out some more salad ingredients to keep the supply going. Spinach beet and sea kale may also be put out.

In the early hours of the 4th the Moon passes into Libra allowing you to move into your fruit producing areas. Expect to be busy here because July is such a demanding period where all fruit trees and bashes are concerned. Many of the following will want harvesting — apples, pears, cherries, gooseberries, currants and whatever else you may have in your particular set-up. After picking, thin out and prune trees and bushes where needed. Deal with all bug infestation efficiently and now — not later.

Once the Moon has passed into Scorpio on the evening of the 6th you should pay attention to the herbs in your garden. They have a huge variety of uses and because of the many new or foreign cooking systems that are so widely available today it now pays to grow your own more than ever. The best time to harvest any herb is while it is still young unless otherwise advised.

However, when you do pick your herbs try to do so while the Moon is waxing to the full and, if possible always while the Moon is in a dry sign (Aries, Gemini, Leo, Sagittarius or

Aquarius), preferably in the first or second quarters.

While the Moon transits Sagittarius from the 9th check through for pests, bugs and vermin and destroy what you find with whatever you have to hand. In particular, especially during July, look for cabbage butterfly eggs on the underside of leaves. These may be crushed or killed with DDT.

Once the Moon is in Capricorn from the 11th you may sow or plant out more carrots, parsnips, radishes, swedes and turnips. As the Moon becomes full on the 12th remember to pick a few mushrooms. If your present supply is getting a tad short this is a perfect time to begin a new bed altogether.

Once their bed has been created mushrooms need very little attention. Try to make your new bed indoors under cover or build one against a north facing wall. It should be around 50 to 70 centimetres in depth but as wide or as long as you wish. Spend this starting time carefully and you will be well rewarded when you come to harvest them.

As the Moon travels through Aquarius from the 13th use the time to clean through greenhouses, sweep drives and pathways, clear out underneath hedges and water everywhere well but sparingly. Pay some attention to the tops of walls where there may be no plant life except for weeds and things. A clean top here always gives that extra "bling" to the garden areas.

The Moon pushes on into Pisces on the 15th which is when you should pay heed to your strawberry beds. Your new beds should be dug in well, apply plenty of manure and throw in some bone meal for good measure. Flowers planted from seed almost always flourish well if put in about now.

The Moon, in her last quarter from the 19th, enters Taurus on the same day. Sow broccoli, cabbage, winter cabbage and parsley. You can put in endive and some cauliflower won't hurt about now either. As there could be a dry spell at any time during this month it will pay you to water well everywhere but do so gently. If you have the time as you make your rounds keep an eye open everywhere and make things as clean and as tidy as possible.

The Moon moves into Cancer on the 24th so it will be time to get busy in among your flower beds, the fruit trees and bushes and anywhere else you see that will warrant your attention. Tie back your young dahlias because the winds may have disturbed them. As you dead head lilies remember to extract the seeds before disposing of the old flower. Cut roses for display indoors, weed and trim alpines Trim and clean out under hedges, tidy up bushes and run your eye over your herb section.,

Renew pond water carefully and slowly using the methods outlined elsewhere. Thoroughly clean out and refresh all the watering holes kept for the visiting animal life. While at this task it wouldn't hurt to the same for their feeding areas either. The birds will be most grateful for many will want to bring their young with them to show them how to find their food. Do the same for your visiting land creatures as well that come by day — like the squirrels. Your night visitors, foxes, or even badgers at times, will also be grateful.

The Moon moves on into Leo on the 26th in the mid afternoon and becomes full very late into the evening. There may be a hint of a tad more than a chill at night these days so it won't hurt to transfer a few plants into boxes, frames or pots — just in case,

Some gardeners will have a few grapes in their greenhouses and these will need to be trimmed and thinned in places. If you have heavy crop tomatoes they also will need similar treatment. And if you have to water in the greenhouse do so carefully at this time of the year.

We often suffer a few heavy downpours — some totally

out of the blue and without any warning — in these final few days of July. Keep a "weather" eye open, just in case because with the Moon entering an earth sign (Virgo) on the 29th this could be a strong possibility.

# August
☀

This is a funny old month because there is no really set pattern to which you need seriously stick and yet there is so much to do. More importantly perhaps, this is often the best time for most folk to go on holiday and then hope that whoever you asked to mow the lawn and water the rest of your garden actually does so while you are away.

In August you need not only to keep picking away from your vegetable patches harvesting in all your goodies you must also plan out where you are going sow or plant fresh or even completely new stock. As it is now high summer this is a good time to harvest cabbage, marrow and courgettes. Pick beans as fast as you can and, if there are too many to eat within a few days or so pick them for freezing.

As August rumbles on it is always a good time to lift onions as gently as you can from the soil, prepare and dry them. If you do this properly they will stay reasonable for as long as you store them well. Beetroot will need to be harvested and, as you gather in cucumbers, check them over. If they show signs of not being as good as they have been in the past it is time to get rid of all your early plantings and get ready to develop what you have growing in frames elsewhere.

Potatoes and tomatoes should still be giving a good yield at this time of the year so feel free to pick and use as you see fit. Later in the month you can always make a fresh planting or sowing along with a fairly large array of other vegetables as well.

Fresh planting and sowing will now need to be carried out. More lettuce won't hurt nor will seeds of spring cabbage and ordinary onions for planting out in the early part of next year. You may also sow a few spring onions along with some Brussels sprouts. Winter spinach and spinach-beet may also be sown for winter use.

Early in the month a few carrots may be sown in sheltered spots and a little more lettuce won't hurt nor will a few more radishes. Mustard and cress will survive as will endive. As long as these sowings are well protected they should all serve you well as their time comes along. Should you decide to sow a little more tomato and cucumber then for best results you should keep them at a regular temperature preferably under glass.

In the fruit garden you will need to pick apples, pears, loganberries and what few grapes that ought to be ready although it may be a tad early for these. Prune raspberries as they finish and turn your attention to pick off some of the late strawberries. Cherries and plums should be at their best by now and a few early melons should be available about now.

All damaged fruit and vegetables should be thrown into the compost heap as long as there is no evidence of pest damage. Where this is so then throw them away or destroy them so whatever the animal may be it won't be able to work its magic in the compost.

If a few strawberries are planted out about now, try not to keep them too close to each other. Place them at least

45 centimetres apart as long as you have the space. Other stronger growing strawberry plants may be in pots and can be forced under glass for next spring use.

In among the flower beds there is much to maintain rather than start or pick anything because the winds are liable to become a little stronger now which can cause quite a few headaches. Growths of all kinds should be thinned carefully this month and plants that need to be tied should all have their ties checked thoroughly and adjusted where necessary.

Plant or replant irises, cut gladiola for indoor display, attend to all roses for many will need to be removed as they fade as the month wears on. Disbud dahlias, spray all flowers against infestation especially in among the pinks and carnations. Remove the supports from any herbaceous border flowers that have finished flowering.

Lift the remaining flower bulbs that are left and prepare to plant out daffodil bulbs for next year. Also, colchicum, autumn flowering crocus and hardy cyclamen should be put out this month. Madonna lily bulbs must be planted in August unlike the other varieties of lily plants. Border carnations layered earlier can now be rooted out and planted where you want them. In the colder areas it might be preferable to put them in pots.

Alpine plants should be sprayed, thinned and any cuttings you want you should take now. In ponds and pools the larger water lilies may need to have a few of their huge leaves cut away to give the rest of the life in there a better chance. Trim hedges and always hoe and weed where you can get in at their bases for these growths should be maturing quite handsomely by now.

Lawns should be checked out for many little patches begin to appear about now and must be renewed. Dig out the bad areas gently, apply a little compost, sow grass seeds, thumb them in firmly then apply plenty of fertiliser about 10 days later. If rainfall seems to be fairly regular, no matter heavy or light it may be, the lawn may not be watered as regularly or separately at this time of the year. When you mow, however, let the clippings stay on the lawn for they will act as a mulch to help retain water.

As before, these tasks for the month ahead are not complete because it isn't possible to think of and get everything carried out properly. In August there is much to do and if you holiday at this time then the work won't be finished as one might wish. The astrological advice given here must also be taken in much the same way. Where you can, keep to the days and times because while it is important to do so it isn't always that simple or easy either.

## August 2014

This month the Moon becomes void-of-course all day on the 2nd, the afternoon of the 6th and the morning of the 7th, the morning of the 9th, 11th and 13th, the afternoon of the 17th, and all day on the 22nd, 24th and 27th. There are a couple of short periods but they may be safely ignored.

There is no proper or set pattern as to how one should try to do this or that because this month is the peak holiday period. Much of what you might normally do may have to be put on hold. A good neighbour may well water your garden for you but he or she may not want or be able to pursue anything else while you are away.

So, during August do what you have to do. If possible pick away in your vegetable patches reaping in what needs to be gathered and, while you are at it plan out where you are going sow or plant fresh or even completely new stock for the new year.

As this is now the peak of summer it is a good time to harvest courgettes, marrow and cabbage. Check your beans daily and pick them off as fast as you can. If you have a fair amount and cannot eat them all in a few days or so then pick them and freeze them.

On the 1st the Moon enters Libra, followed by Scorpio on the 3rd. Both tomatoes and potatoes will be flourishing well giving good yields now — pick and use as you deem fit.

Later on you may make fresh planting or sowing along with lettuce, spring cabbage for planting out in the early in the next year. Sow some sprouts, early spinach and spinach-beet. Sow some carrots where there is good shelter. Do this along with radishes, mustard and cress and endive. Protect such sowing well and they should all flourish when their time comes. A few more cucumbers and tomatoes under glass may be sown and kept under glass at a fixed temperature.

The Moon, now in her first quarter, moves into Sagittarius on the 5th when a few more ordinary onions, spring onions and even a few late leeks and shallots could be sown or planted. Root growth plants do well if put out under this Moon.

Capricorn hosts the new Moon from the 7th when any further cutting, pruning or grafting exercises may be undertaken. Around now is about the right time for planting autumn flowering crocuses and cyclamen.

The Moon moves on into Aquarius on the 9th. Any damaged fruit and vegetables ought not to be put into your composter where there is obvious damage from pests. It is wiser to do this than simply throw them away. Destroy them so whatever damage has been done can't be extended to anything else.

The Moon enters Pisces on the 11th around noon. Strong strawberry growths may be put into pots to be forced under glass for next year. In the flower areas there is much work to keep you going rather than start anything anew. Check ties where they are in use and adjust accordingly

You should now replant irises and a few gladioli for a display in the house. Check your roses thoroughly, deadhead and remove where it is needed. Dahlias should be disbudded and all flowers ought to be sprayed against pest damage as a matter of course, especially carnations and the pinks.

The Moon moves on into Aries on the 13th and about time for another bonfire. Now you can really destroy all unwanted waste but do remember to keep the ashes for use later. Once again, have a clear out, clean tools, edge paths, check drainage systems and run water around guttering and down pipes to ensure they are working properly

Once the Moon has moved into Taurus on the 15th you should check lawns for those irritating little patches that seem to just suddenly appear. Clear the areas, apply some compost with a bit of ash from your recent bonfire, press in the new seed and some fertiliser. The lawn will want watering regularly and, when you mow, let the clippings lie for they will help as mulch to retain the water.

The Moon moves on into Cancer on the 20th. Spray, thin and take any take cuttings from your alpines. Large water lilies and excess growth of anything else in your pond will need to be cut back to give the animal life some relief. Trim hedges and hoe and weed under them.

After the Moon moves into Virgo on the 25th it is worth lifting the flower bulbs you have left. This would also be a good time to plant daffodil along with autumn flowering crocus, colchicum, and cyclamen. Madonna lily bulbs should be planted this month. Also, root out border carnations layered earlier and plant them where you want them. If the weather is too cool put them in pots or a while.

The now new Moon enters Libra quite late on the evening of the 27th which is a signal for you to put in a few seeds of winter lettuce; prepare the selected patch for planting spring cabbage. For those who have space a green crop may now put out in vacant ground. Dig it well in so that the frost doesn't get there before you.

Once the Moon has moved on into Scorpio on the 30th gather up all your waste green material, and other dead or dying growths and put in your compost heap — add water and or sulphate of ammonia to get all going. Turn it all over regularly to ensure all of it rots reasonably evenly.

These tasks for August are not the be-all and end-all of what you can and should do but with the annual holidays likely to interfere it simply isn't possible get everything carried out properly. There is so much to this month not everything will be completed satisfactorily.

It is much the same with my astrological notes for, while they have been created properly, a few liberties have been taken with some of the timing. .As to whether you can maintain all or any of these suggestions, while it is important to do so it isn't always that simple or easy either.

# September

❄

Autumn has arrived and with it an occasional sample of much cooler nights but still with a few rather nice summer daytime periods. It is time to clear away the remains of any plant life that has now finished for the year. Cuttings should be taken from shrubs and selected flowers of your choice. Where possible, really clean through as much as possible, sweep the lawn, all the paths, the drive and the edges of the green areas where they lay against walls.

Before the really cold weather arrives have all your electricity arrangements properly checked over by a professional if you can't do it yourself. Cabling and weather-proofing involving these installations can start to lose their efficacy after the summer and at the start of damp cold nights the last thing anyone wants is a power failure at the first sign of a frosty spell.

Drains and gutters need to be totally cleaned through so that all debris is moved out and you should run your hose through them to make sure you have cleared it all. If you have any need to work on major changes — anything from slightly re-designing the shape of your garden to laying concrete, re-building or extending walls or the paving perhaps then the early part of this month is the best time for such activities. Remember, concrete that has been affected by frost will simply fall apart once it has warmed up again.

When you clip your hedges ensure you pull all weeds from the ground but don't just leave them lying on the ground for they are liable to root again. Either destroy them in a small bonfire along with any other rubbish you need to dispose of or throw them on the compost heap. If you are planning any extra hedges, lengthening or strengthening present ones now is the time to get things ready but not for planting just yet because the ground should be left for several months.

Indoor plants should be moved away from window areas at night but you may still allow them all the light they want during the day time. Indoor temperatures are usually fairly static but even plants like to move with the times. Remove the faded or weakening plants, empty the pots and refill with fresh soil and a little manure. On outdoor patios much the same should be carried out here as well. If you throw away old flowers empty those containers too but refill and prepare for planting spring bulbs. If you aren't going to use any of the containers empty them and store until wanted again.

And while on the subject of light September is an excellent month in which to create a new indoor mushroom bed. Although they may be grown almost anywhere now is certainly a splendid period in which to create a new bed for if started about now mid-October will see your first pickings which could last easily well into winter. Cover well with straw and keep lighting to a minimum for mushrooms grow best in the dark.

Vegetables like spring cabbage may be planted out and lettuce sown in a frame should help the winter supply somewhat. Prick out red cabbage if you sowed any last month. Move parsley from the July sowing and transplant them along with a few french beans for forcing later.

Elsewhere, it is advisable to harvest other vegetables and certainly fruit should be gathered in now before frosts, if any, start to appear again. So, pick off apples and pears as they become ready, prune blackberries and peaches and tie the growths back well to protect against possible high winds.

It is a good idea to have a thorough clean-up in among the fruit trees and bushes, clear away the deadwood, rake up the leaves and hoe ready for new plantings of cane fruits like currants and gooseberries.

At this time of the year because of the dampness about mildew is a danger for all plants although it should be possible for you to ease the problem by spraying a good fungicide that has been created for this purpose. Alternatively, and especially indoors, a dry atmosphere may see an increase in red spider infestation. Once again use a spray where you can that has been created for this work as well. There are some people who swear by spreading cigarette, pipe and or cigar ash over their webs. They claim this will also get rid of the little pests but, I would ask, where do they then go?

Much of the rest of the suggested work is more or less looking ahead. Early bulbs like scillas and pots of crocus are always welcome sights in the deep of winter so now is a very good time to place corms or bulbs in their pots. Cuttings of bedding fuchsia and geraniums should be taken about this time of the year for they will root readily in pots or a well-protected garden frame.

Plant out daffodil and narcissus bulbs now for they will become quite strong and ready for your next year showing. Along with these you may also pot on or put in bowls all spring flowering bulbs. By all means leave them in the garden for a few more weeks but if it looks like being really frosty bring them in or put them in the greenhouse.

You may have to begin to keep a watchful eye on your overnight heating arrangements in the green house now because the nights, if not frosty, will certainly be damp by the time morning arrives. Heavy dew is almost always expected as the month wears on and you will see evidence of this when you move outside in the early hours.

And please try to remember to make sure any water and food containers for the visiting wild life are kept clean and full.

All the tasks referred to here for September are fairly extensive but as before, they cannot cover all that has to be done. The astrological advice however, while pertinent and to the point may also be a tad limited so in the paragraphs that follow on you will be given guidance as to when you should carry out these tasks in line with the phase and position of the Moon but even this is not complete either. Once again, because it isn't mentioned doesn't mean you should not attempt the tasks.

## September 2014

As far as the gardener is concerned, the Moon is void-of-course this September all day on the 11th, the afternoon of the 13th, the morning of the 16th and 21st, the afternoon of the 23rd and all day on the 30th.

As the month opens the Moon is in her last quarter in Scorpio. She enters Sagittarius later the same day in the afternoon at about 17.15 hours and becomes new the following morning.

Cooler nights will now be upon us although during the day it is still pleasant and usually quite warm. Start September by taking any cuttings you want from your flowers and shrubs. Have a good sweep up everywhere, the pathways, drive, the edges of the lawn and, indeed, even the lawn itself.

Remove all the debris from drains, guttering and any other cleaning system you have in your garden. Everything needs to be checked and cleared out because quite soon now the leaves will start to fall and they can create all sorts of problems if left for too long. Run your hose through all your pipe works to be sure it has all been cleared.

Now is a good time to start work any major changes you want to put in. Lay concrete, extend paving and or walls or re-build where you deem it is needed. Don't forget that concrete affected by frost will start to show holes or just fall apart once it has warmed up again.

Also, this is a good opportunity to check over all of your electric apparatus and tools, if needs be, by a professional if you are unable to do it. You will have been hard at work using these materials all through the summer and have probably only paid lip service to keeping them up to scratch. Weather proofing and cabling loses its efficacy as the autumn weeks wear on. When the damp or cold nights arrive the last thing you will want is a power failure at the first sign of frost.

The Moon enters Pisces on the 7th. Lettuce may be sown in a frame to help your supply through the winter or at least up until Christmas. Spring cabbage may be planted and do remember to prick out any red cabbage that you may have sown last month. Parsley should be moved from where you sowed it in July and transferred along with a few french beans to be forced later.

This is an ideal time to really look ahead and put out early daffodil and narcissus bulbs as this will give them plenty of strength for next year If you have the time pot on (or put in bowls) any spring flower bulbs. They can be left for a little while longer as long as you keep an eye on the coming weather. At the first sign of frost bring them indoors or in the greenhouse.

The Moon moves on into Aries late in the evening of the 9th. It is never too early to ensure that you maintain an adequate overnight heating in all greenhouses now because the nights can be quite cold, if not frosty

The early part of the month may well be a tad damp by dawn. There is almost always a heavy dew in most areas from the early nights of September and if you go outside early enough you'll see this for yourself. And may I remind you to please ensure that water and food containers put out for visiting wild life are kept clean and full.

Taurus hosts the Moon from the 12th and, as this month is a good time to start a mushroom bed you should see to it about now. Mushrooms may be grown virtually anywhere and if you like them you can be eating them by the middle of next month and possibly, all through the winter depending the weather and where you put them. Keep them well covered preferably in the dark.

Once the Moon has moved into Gemini on the 14th will be a good time to look at indoor and patio plants. Because temperatures can vary it might be an idea to move your indoor flowers away from the windows during the night hours but they may be put back during the day.

The Moon enters Cancer on the 16th. Dispose of any faded or weakening plants, empty their pots and top them up with fresh soil and manure.

Do the same for the outdoor patio growths as well. Here too you may throw out the old flowers and empty their containers. However, there is no need to refill or prepare them unless you are going to use them for planting spring bulbs, otherwise once emptied they can be put into store until wanted again.

Once the Moon has moved into Virgo on the 21st put in a few cuttings of heliotrope for they will root quite well in frame or box in the greenhouse and, if possible, use sandy compost. Check over the herb garden and gather in what needs to be harvested preferably at the times suggested earlier but if not, now is a good a time as ever.

The Moon enters Libra on the 24th. Pot out schizanthus one per small pot and put them near the edge of the greenhouse where they can take in all the light they love so much. Do the same with cyclamen but use compost of a leaf and peat mix and put them in a frame.

Once the Moon has passed into Scorpio on the 26th take cuttings of calceolarias and penstemons and place them in a frame in sandy soil. Check out apple and pears because they tend to become ready at quite different times.

It will be necessary to harvest them as and when they each become ready. If a fruit comes away in your hand reasonably easily, it is ready. Also, when you decide to clip through your hedges do make sure that all the weeds are pulled right out of the ground or they will simply take root again.

When you do pull them don't just leave them lying about but gather them up and destroy them by fire along with any other rubbish you need to get rid of or throw them on the compost heap.

Continue on until the end of the month.

# October

✹

Like most months, October depends quite a lot on the level of weather in respect of what we should be able to do or not do at any time. When it is all boiled down very little actual planting or sowing really takes place this month for it is very much a period of cleaning and maintaining what we have rather than actually starting anything new in the real sense.

The days seem to be getting shorter much faster and on Sunday 26th at 02.00 hours we put the clocks back one hour here in the UK. That is, of course, unless the government has decided otherwise between now (the time of writing) and then. Having said that we shall deal first with what we can plant or sow in each of the three fields of vegetables, fruit and flowers. We can look at alpines, herbs, lawns, hedges, trees, bushes and ponds later.

This is the last month in which one may reasonably expect any substantial growth but it is still possible to put out a few late sowings of french beans and even a few peas under cloches. Some authorities recommend the planting of spring cabbages from the August seed growing exercise so if you feel your growths are ready plant them along with a few winter and spring lettuce under glass. It won't hurt to put in a few more of the larger size of radish while you are at it.

Gather in the last of your runner beans — and you can use two methods here. The larger pod should be saved for immediate use while the smaller ones should be prepared, frozen and stored for later use. If there are any others let them turn colour as they will then you may cut them all down and compost them later in the month. Cut remaining marrows if you have them, lift the last of your beetroot and bring indoors any remaining tomatoes.

Gather up the potatoes that are near maturity and if you have any carrots left it would be best to take them out now. Unless you have other special vegetables left which are not mentioned here you ought to gather them in before the frosts arrive or the ground gets too hard to manage properly.

In among the fruit trees and bushes you need to make your final forays in respect of apples and pears. Prune peaches and cut away basal growths of raspberries and, after pruning where necessary, tie back cherries. This is also the time to prune blackberries and cut back shoots on the weaker looking growths. Once these tasks are completed you may clear away all the debris that has mounted up, dig over soil and prepare the ground for planting gooseberries, currants and cane fruits as, when and where you want them.

In your flower beds it is time to be much more severe than you have been for you must cut and remove all fading annuals before they become too bedraggled for anything. While colour as such does not have to completely disappear from your garden you will have to lift, repot or remove so many different plants that there simply isn't enough space to list them all here. However, once you have finalised what you are going to do it will then be time to dig over all the bare patches and either redesign the garden or get all the areas ready for sowing and planting later.

If you have any alpines ready either as seedlings or as rooted cuttings now is the time to plant them except for anything you may have in pots which can be kept back. But if you are tight for space in your greenhouse, shed or any room in the house where you might keep such things then put them in to gain the space back. Where herbs are concerned you might want to take a few more cuttings of bay, rue and for the very clever gardener, some lavender for this is one very difficult plant with which to experiment.

A few roots of parsley lifted now with plenty of soil still attached may be transferred and placed in a frame for winter use. Dig up some fennel for you to force later in your greenhouse. And, of course, most of the time you should always have a little mint handy so you could divide a few roots for planting or potting in a warmer place.

Lawns will need a really expert touch about now. If they are well trodden in they need to be properly aerated either with the correct tool or with whatever you might have to hand. Grass may be allowed to grow to around no higher than 5 to 7 centimetres or so now — it won't hurt but any unsightly patches will and they should be properly repaired.

Keep off the lawn as much as you can after you have worked over the areas that need treatment and then cover with an autumn fertiliser. If you have a flat lawn try to ensure that the drainage arrangements will be sufficient for the coming winter period. Those that slope slightly will drain well as a rule.

We turn now to your hedges where, if you are going to add any growth to strengthen, lengthen or divide areas you will need to put in deciduous plants before the end of the month. Evergreens should be planted in by mid-month at the latest.

This list of tasks for October is relatively short for not a lot happens in the sowing or planting fields. However, a lot of cleaning, clearing and tidying up does and the jobs listed here really are far from complete because most individual plants and other growths are all treated differently. Thus, this really is only a guide. All the astrological data suggested for you to time your efforts with the phase and position of the Moon is not that complete either. Please remember, because it isn't mentioned in doesn't mean you should not carry out such tasks.

This month calls more for straightening out with only a few planting or sowing exercises and, for as long as you are careful in how or what you are cleaning at the time, you should have little trouble.

## October 2014

This month there are not so many void-of-course Moon periods so we can get quite a lot of work done. At the best of times October is always a busy four weeks or so for any gardener and we will need all the time we can get to achieve all of our aims.

The Moon becomes void-of-course on the afternoon of the 8th, the morning of the 9th and the 11th, the afternoon of the 18th, the morning of the 21st and the morning of the 30th. She is in her first quarter when she enters Capricorn early on the 1st.

The next few weeks or so are more or less the last where we might reasonably expect any real growth although we may still but put in a few late sowings of french beans and even a few peas under cloches. There are those who suggest we may plant out spring cabbages from our earlier August seed growing exercise. Check them over and if you think they are ready then by all means plant them along with a few winter and spring lettuce under glass. It won't hurt to put in a few more of the larger size of radish while you are at it.

The Moon moves on into Aquarius on the 3rd. All lawns will be ready for the more thorough touch at this time. Most are likely to be well well-trodden in and should be properly aerated with the proper tool for the job. However, if you have a suitable alternative please feel free to use it. You can now let your grass grow to around no higher than 7-10 centimetres or so. This won't hurt its appearance but any patches that have not been attended to will. Repair them now.

Once you have carried out these small but necessary tasks try to stay off the lawn as much as possible, Cover them with an autumn fertiliser and ensure your drainage system not only works but will last the coming four or five months of cold weather. Generally speaking, if your lawn has a slight slope to it all should be well but, nevertheless, play safe and keep an eye on it — just in case

The Moon enters Pisces on the 5th. Your flower beds must now be assessed and where it is obviously needed you must be quite resolute. Remove all the fading annuals before they become unusable for anything. Colour is nice but selective cutting should still allow a reasonable display.

Nothing has to completely disappear as such but you are going to have to remove or lift and repot so many different plants there simply isn't enough space to list them all.

However, once you have finalised what you are going to do the Moon moving into Aries on the 7th now permits you to dig all the open patches which may allow you to rethink where you will put all your new planting and sowing in the coming few months.

The (by now) full Moon enters Taurus on the 9th. Check over your alpine section and if you have anything ready as rooted cuttings or as seedlings by all means plant them except for anything you may have in pots which ought to be kept back. However, if space is limited in your garden shed, greenhouse or where you might keep things indoors then put them in as well to claw back some of this space.

Once the Moon moves into Gemini on the 11th take a more thorough survey of your hedges where, if you are going to add anything to divide up, lengthen or strengthen them make a note of what you decide and be ready to put in this deciduous plant life before the end of October. Plant out any evergreens the end of the next week at the latest.

The Moon moves on into Cancer very late on the 13th. Have a good look around your fruit bushes and trees especially where the last of your apples and pears ought to be still ripening. Cut away the base of your raspberries, prune peaches and, after pruning where your black cherries are, remember to tie them back carefully. While you are at it you should do the same for your blackberries. By all means cut back the weaker growths.

Once the Moon has entered Leo on the 16th have a good clean up and clear away the debris that has bound to have mounted up. Prepare the ground and dig up the soil for where you will eventually plant your new cane fruits, currants and gooseberries as and when and where you will want them.

The Moon passes into Virgo on the 18th. Lift the ripe marrows and store them well away from any frost that could attack them. Gather in your main crop potatoes, look them over and dispose of anything that looks suspicious. It would be a good time about now to pick off the last of your runner beans. Use the larger one more of less straightaway but cut, prepare and freeze the smaller ones.

The Moon moves into Libra on the 21st and you should use the time to take a good look over your herb garden. Take a few cuttings of bay, rue and, if you feel up to the challenge do the same with some lavender — a most difficult plant with which to experiment.

Once the Moon passes into Scorpio on the 23rd lift a few roots of parsley and put them in a frame for later use. Fennel taken now may be forced later in your greenhouse. Don't forget you should always have a little mint handy. Divide a few roots for planting or potting on in a warmer place.

After the Moon enters Capricorn on the 28th sow a few peas under cloches in flat bottom drills. Sow your seed around 9-10 centimetres apart, but not more than three or four rows at a time because they love the space.

The clocks go back ("fall" back) on the 26th.

As an alternative to animal manure your compost may be used. Compost heaps created earlier in the year should be given a thorough turning over so that the outer material is back fair and square in the centre and then you may use as much as you want as you see fit.

# November

❖

As the days have very definitely started to draw in and the nights are not only (seemingly) darker and longer they are very much colder too. However, there are a few good moments because November often gives us a few rather nice warm reminders of summer days – albeit not for long. Despite this the rainfall is usually heavy but, for as long as the rain does fall it isn't cold enough for frost.

So much can be and is achieved during the next few weeks that we will start with the fruit tree and bush areas. Plant new apples and pear trees and, if necessary, either remove old trees or severely prune them back. If needs be put in supports for small or very young trees. Plant out new red currant, blackcurrant and gooseberry bushes. It is wiser to not prune peach, cherry, damson or plum trees this month.

On the vegetable scene fresh broad beans may be sown under glass and a few lettuces may also be sown out. A few shallots wouldn't hurt about now along with a handful or so of horse-radish roots. The adventurous gardener may also experiment with a few hardy peas — but in a sheltered position or the frost will kill them. Lift a few parsnips and, if you have any, pick savoy cabbages and be selective if you have any sprouts still outside that can be harvested.

In both the fruit and vegetable areas where you either cannot do any anymore or there is no room at present now is a good time to turn over soil before it gets too claggy for easy digging. Once a few frosts have hardened the top soil it is quite a job to get a fork or spade into these surfaces. So, if the weather is still reasonable these tasks will lighten your working load considerably if carried out about now.

Try to spread some lime and a little leaf mould although if you have no lime available at the moment then use manure but don't use the two together for they act against each other. When or if you do manage to dig anywhere really go quite deep for the more you expose the under-soil the more there is for the elements to get at and refresh.

In the flower beds there is much that may be planted or sown out this month. Herbaceous borders may be put out and tulips for flowering around May of next year. Divide ferns and remove gladiola corms for storage, plant hyacinths under glass and pot on lily-of-the-valley. Many gardeners choose now to plant new roses because it does give them time to mature and become well established. Prick out a few sweet pea seedlings from your October exercises and pot on under glass.

There are a wide ranging number of other flowers that gardeners will put out this month but they vary from area to area. What may be planted or sown in the south may not survive in the north, and parts of the east are far wetter than in the west. Your locale determines the way you should work in this area. However, when you are not putting out fresh stock you should at least be preparing the beds for when you can or will be doing so.

It is important to thoroughly check over water plants, pools and ponds for they must be looked at this month especially where there are fallen leaves to be cleared away.

Nets across the tops of all ponds are a help but they must be cleaned off regularly. While they are left there leaves and other debris could start to rot and if any of this passes through to fall into the water your fish are liable to suffer from poisoning.

A good job now would be to check over any water pumps that you may have. It isn't a particularly nice job but it doesn't take long. Curiously, this also a very easy job to tackle, even for amateurs. Thin out reeds and water plants generally.

Alpines and rock gardens should also be looked over. You may plant small shrubs and heathers and put hardy pot plants in if you wish. Trim and deadhead where needed and remember to save the seeds because this part of the exercise alone can save gardener quite a few pennies. Dress the rockery area with small shingle, coloured pebbles or whatever suits you.

We touched on lawns and their care last month, but in November a few unsightly spots might still need to be cleared away. Incidentally, the amount of worm casts that can and often do appear overnight should not come as a surprise because, if nothing else, this tells you the soil is in good condition but the worms are spoiling the surface somewhat. Aerate the surface yet again with whatever you have to hand then use a good strong wire rake rather than the traditional metal version. Brush it all over well afterwards and the lawn will take care of itself for a while.

At this time of the year it never hurts to completely clear out the greenhouse and give it a good clean. Grease the doors and window hinges, repair holes if there are any and make sure that when it is all back together again there are no nasty draughts anywhere. As you put your greenery back in you can decide what you want to keep or throw because you never really get around to doing this while it is all in there. Water your indoor plant life sparingly.

As usual, the rather varied tasks listed here for November are far from complete because so much varies depending on where you live. During the winter period the differences between the north, south east and west can be strong so this really can only be a guide for this month. The astrologically based thinking for what work to do and when really does need to be timed properly. The positions and phases of the Moon are complete but, just because it may not be mentioned it does not mean you should not carry out such tasks.

## November 2014

This month the Moon becomes void-of-course all day on the 1st and 3rd, the afternoon of the 5th, all day on the 12th and 17th, the afternoon of the 19th, the morning of the 22nd and all day on the 24th and is waxing to the full when she moves into Pisces late on the afternoon of the 1st.

Gardeners have a lot of flowers to plant or sow this month. Put out tulips for flowering around late April or early May, and do the same in your herbaceous borders. At about now one ought to remove any gladiola corms and store for later use. Pot on lily-of-the-valley, divide ferns and plant a few hyacinths under glass. It depends on who or where you are but many gardeners choose this time to plant new roses to allow them plenty of time to establish and become mature.

You could also prick out a few sweet pea seedlings and pot on but under glass or they won't survive. What is planted in or sown in the north is not the same as in the south because the weather can differ quite a bit this month. If you choose not to put in any fresh growths at this time you could at least prepare the beds you will want to use later on.

The Moon enters Aries on the 3rd. If you are unable to do anymore planting or sowing for whatever reasons cast your eye over your fruit and vegetable areas. Begin digging and turn the present much softer soil before it gets claggy and hard to use. After a frost or two has firmed up the earth it will need quite an effort to get your fork to work the ground as you would wish. So, as long as the weather remains reasonable these tasks will lighten the load quite considerably.

While you are at it you should throw lime and leaf mould over the patch once you have finished digging. If you don't have any lime do use ordinary manure but don't add lime later for they are not compatible.

If you should decide to work over the earth get your fork or shovel down really deep because the deeper you delve the more under soil you will bring up and there will be for the elements to get at.

The Moon moves on into Taurus on the evening of the 5th. It may sound a tad strange for the time of the year but about now a few lettuces may be sown out and fresh broad beans can be sown, under glass, of course. A few radish roots and some shallots won't hurt now either.

If you want to tempt the fates try putting in some hardy peas in a sheltered position away from and real or severe frost that could occur. Pull parsnips and if you have any do the same with savoy cabbages. It will pay to be selective if you harvest a few sprouts that you may still have outside.

The Moon enters Gemini on the 8th. If you have time use it to clean out the greenhouse. While you are at it oil the window and door catches and try to make good all the little bits of damage that will have mounted up somewhat in the past few weeks. Repair all the little holes if there are any and ensure that when you have gone through everything there won't be any draughts to spoil any plant growth put in later.

When you do put things back decisions will have to be made as to what you will keep and what should be thrown because it simply isn't possible to do so when your greenhouse is full up. Once everything has been put back to your satisfaction you may water all your indoor life but sparingly.

The Moon enters Cancer on the evening of the 10th. Ponds, pools and other water attractions in your particular garden must now have a pretty good check – if nothing else, at least clean away the fallen leaves. Even if you have a net spread across the surface which is quite a good help most of the time they should still cleaned regularly.

Leaves that are allowed to rot may pass through the netting and fall into the water and that means real trouble for whatever life that exists in there. While they are left there leaves and other debris could start to rot and if any of this passes through to fall into the water your fish are liable to suffer from poisoning.

The Moon moves into Leo on the 12th which is an ideal period to check over any electrical machinery and tools you may have. Continue with your pond work and give any water pumps a check and a clean. It may not be a nice job as such but has to be done and it isn't too hard a task even for an amateur. When you replace the pump(s) take the opportunity to thin out reeds and other over grown water plants.

The Moon pushes on into Scorpio on the 20th. Turn now to your alpine and or rock garden. They will need some attention and perhaps a few additions to the life already there. Small shrubs, heathers and even a couple of hardy pot plants wouldn't hurt. Deadhead and trim to your heart's content but do keep the seeds because they will save you money if you keep them to use as when later on. When you have finished all these little tasks throw a few handfuls of small coloured pebbles or shingles to give it that extra good look.

The Moon moves into Capricorn on the 24th. The fruit trees and bushes may be cut back, pruned or even replaced where you might think it necessary. New apple and pear trees may be needed and make a point to double-check supports for any small or very young trees.

Put in fresh black and red currant bushes along with new gooseberry bushes. It is not a good idea to prune peach, cherry, damson or plum trees during November.

After the Moon enters Aquarius on the evening of the 26th make a point of looking at what you might not have done because of the weather which can and does often spring a few surprises at this time of the year.

The nights are really drawing in now and it can be definitely much colder. There may also be a few good moments too — the rather nice warm days although as a rule not for long. And then there are the rainy days. However, if it does rain then remember that it isn't cold enough for frost.

# December

❄

The middle of winter is more or less upon us now and what with the night frosts the garden looks a tad bare when you think of what it did look like back in the middle of summer. There is very little to try to plant or sow this month and what you already have growing must be well protected from night frosts — but just precisely where to start is the main question of any day.

For those of you with fish in their ponds it is time to take action not only against ice and snow but also that the water surface is kept completely free of all debris of any kind. Clean off the surface, drain out some of the water and refill slowly by laying the hose along the side of the pond allowing a steady flow.

Once you have refilled it place several rubber balls of any size on the water and leave them. If or when the water should freeze the balls will absorb the pressure and all you have to do remove them and the small holes left become breathing spaces for the fish.

Never break any icy surface by hitting it. Either lever up from the edge or pour hot water carefully on a weak point to make the ice melt. Hitting the ice over the pond could damage the fish that, incidentally, rarely need feeding in the winter.

If you haven't already done so, now is a good time to spread a small-hole netting system across the pond to keep out fallen leaves, other unwanted debris and any large fish-eating birds like, for example, the heron. These birds are quite adventurous and will try anything to get fish but will not try to get under any netting

We should turn our attention now to the hygiene of the soil and your everyday tools and bits and pieces that have been in use throughout the year. Everything that you might normally use needs to be thoroughly cleaned. Disinfect pots, boxes and containers that you are going to use again. Burn anything that you are going to dispose of in a bonfire but when the fire is out rake up the ashes for spreading on the vegetable patches that you will dig over later.

This is one of the main reasons why gardeners like to rotate their crop areas. If, for example you have grown tomatoes or other vegetable in the same place all year it is possible that the area has become infected with something that regularly attacks that plant — especially when it is always there.

So to plant the same growth again in the same place is often fraught with problems that you do not find out about until it is too late. To prevent this ever happening to you dig over the plot or plots as deeply as you can. Really turn the soil over quite thoroughly. Spread a good store-bought steriliser over the area and leave it alone for at least four or five weeks.

If there is anything there it will be dead by the time you want to use the plot again. If there should still be any vegetable waste to dispose of simply dig it in as you turn over the plots or create trenches.

Among the flowers beds is where you can really set to and produce excellent results through taking cuttings, pruning and even having a few grafting exercises. Cut back chrysanthemums and a little later on after you have given them a chance to recover take a few cuttings.

Prune roses and fruit trees as you see fit. It is an old country custom or saying that fruit trees may not be looked at this at this time of the year so you may safely ignore this old saw.

Gather in a few twigs from the various trees and shrubs, bring them indoors into a warm room and you should have a colourful Christmas when the time comes.

If planting out any shrubs or ornamental trees check out that grease-bands are in place on the older trees. Animals can be destructive at times, especially rabbits and if they attack any of your trees this takes a good early and rather necessary action against them.

Onions sown now in the greenhouse will flourish well under glass and if kept at a steady temperature at around 12° to 15° centigrade. When you venture out to select which evergreen cuttings you are going to have for Christmas decorations use secateurs and cut away where the loss will not be obvious. You may have to be a tad savage when it comes to trimming and cutting back holly trees, bushes or hedges because somehow or other it just grows and grows and gets quite out of hand just when you don't need it.

You will need to continue to look after and keep your herbaceous borders clear. Dig carefully between plants and check for invasive root formations from whatever source. Tree roots tend to search continually for extra food all throughout the year and they can spread to quite a few metres away from their base. Take a sharp blade or keen edged spade and work around your border looking for this type of root. If you do find anything all you have to do is sever it and end will simply just rot and die in the earth.

If the weather is bad enough to stop you working outdoors, use the time to clean, sharpen renew or replace gardens tools and other appliances. Spades should always be sharpened after clearing away the dirt and even rust. Blades of all sorts should be brought up to scratch and if you know how spend some time with your electrical bits and pieces even if you only remove the dirt and other debris.

If you have already worked on this you could spend time looking through your gardening manuals and magazines for a few ideas on what you could place where or to see what is on the market that may be of some use to you.

This month the work is going to be quite varied and not wholly complete because of whatever the weather decides to throw at us. There will be the odd occasion when we could be lucky and have a summery spell of good weather or it will choose to close in so tightly we just can't get outside to get anything done.

So, while the astrological advice given here still stands it too can be subjected to the vagaries of the weather. Try to keep to the days and times as shown because it is important although it may not be possible to carry out them all out as indicated. Alternative days may be used in such circumstances. If you look at all the advice given elsewhere you will soon see what you can or ought not to do at such times.

## December 2014

In this coming month there are several days when the Moon becomes void-of-course. However, and because much of December's work is clearing away and tidying up just do what you can when you can. So, for gardeners, the Moon will be void-of-course all day on the 7th and 17th, the afternoon of the 21st and all day on the 23rd.

As the month opens the waxing to the full Moon is in Aries. Should you be unable to work outdoors it will prove quite helpful for you to look over your tools and at the very least while cleaning them all, you could renew or replace outworn items.

Clean away any rust and sharpen your spades and the blades on the mower. If you are able to do so, then spend time on all with your electrical appliances even if only to clean away the dirt and other debris.

About now is also a very good time to sift through any magazines or manuals you haven't had sufficient time to read properly and see if there aren't a few ideas you could easily use to make life easier in your garden.

The Moon enters Taurus on the 3rd and this will allow you to get among your flowers beds and see where you need to prune, cut and or graft. It wouldn't hurt to cut back any of your chrysanthemums or even prune a few roses that may have got a tad out of hand. There is a very old country saying "prune roses and fruit trees as you see fit" but at this time of the year you may safely ignore anything along these lines.

The Moon moves into Gemini on the 5th. Christmas is only a couple of weeks or so away and now might be a choice time to have a good look around in the garden and collect in all the twigs you will need from the various trees and shrubs. If you bring them in the warmth of indoors now they will prove to be a rather nice decoration for the holiday when the time comes.

The Moon enters Cancer on the 7th. For those of you with fish you must think of what damage snow and ice can do. Take action to ensure that water surfaces are kept completely free of debris of any kind. Clean and drain some of the water away. Refill slowly and, when this has been completed and refill slowly by laying the hose along the side of the pond allowing a steady flow.

Once you have done this, put a few rubber balls of any size on the water and leave them there. Should the water freeze the balls absorb the increased pressure. All you need do is take them out and the small holes they leave become little breathing areas for your pond life.

Incidentally, one should never break an icy surface by hitting it. Pour hot water carefully on to the ice or lever it up by leaving a small branch half in the water and resting on the edge. If you hit the ice on a pond surface it might hurt or damage the fish that rarely need feeding in the winter anyway.

The Moon moves into Leo on the 10th and it's time to renew or create fresh greasebands on both older trees and your newer acquisitions. All the different animal life that come into your garden, whether regular visitors or not can be quite destructive especially the rabbits for they will have a go at any trees. Taking this precaution now is a good insurance against what they will do when they do appear.

After the Moon enters Virgo on the 12th survey the garden and try to work out how you are going to rotate your various growth areas. For example, if you continuously grow the same plant life in the same place each season the area could become infected with something that regularly attacks that particular plant – especially if it is always there.

To prevent this happening in your garden dig over all your plots and delve as deep as you can. After this spread recommended shop-bought steriliser and leave it all alone for at least a month or so. If anything was in there it will be well and truly dead by the time you want to use the plot again.

The Moon moves into Libra on the 15th and then into Scorpio on the 17th. This will give you the opportunity to spread your efforts on a variety of different exercises. To start with trim and cut back your holly trees, bushes and hedges because one way or another such things just grow and grow and can get so out of hand.

Check trees for invasive root formations because tree roots are searching for food all the time. Sometimes these roots can reach up to several metres away. Get a good sharp blade or a keen-edged shovel and if you do find anything along these lines simply sever the offending root.

The Moon ventures into Sagittarius rather late on the evening of the 19th and a few onions sown now will flourish under glass but only if kept at a steady temperature of some 12° to 15° centigrade. Lift roots of mint, put them in a deep seed box and cover with old potting soil. Place them in a frame in the greenhouse and watch for their shoots so you can pick them early.

The Moon enters Capricorn on the 22nd you could begin your preparations for seed sowing in the greenhouse by cleaning all your old boxes and pots, Arrange for supplies of sand, peat and lime to be delivered and, if you have one, check over your warm frame in which to raise your early seedlings.

It is now mid-winter. Night frosts can make any garden look a trifle rough especially when you compare it what you had during the previous summer. There is now really nothing to try to plant or sow this but you already have along these lines must be well protected.

You aren't going to do much more between now and January and away we go again as the new cycle begins.

As a gardener your life is rarely still for long — if at all — and hopefully all this information has been of some help.

# Tips and Wrinkles

❖

This list is not a "be-all and end-all" of lunar gardening philosophy by any means but over the years it has become an invaluable guide with an extremely helpful set of hints which if adopted, will help to achieve that extra edge to your finished holding.

### Aeration

Where possible, and for the best results, try to aerate the soil when the Moon is ascending. Earth and soil will break up much more easily when the Moon is descending.

### Calendar

The weekly, monthly and seasonal calendar we enjoy here in the UK is Sun or solar based. The astrological system that the vast majority of astrologers generally tend to use is Moon or lunar based. The two methods will never meet in our life time although just occasionally the Moon phases do seem to connect with the solar year for a short while. This tends to happen quite often in January when the first day of the year often coincides with the first quarter phase of the

Moon. But that is all it is — pure coincidence.

## Cleaning

The use of insecticides, disinfectants, DDT and all the many other proprietary cleaners have been having a devastating effect on the natural life of plants and animals just about everywhere. When cleaning out in the open, in the greenhouse, the garden shed or even in-doors do try to use natural cleaners wherever possible because these cleaners are creating an imbalance on nature in general. It may seem quite strange to you (at least, until you try them) but ordinary baby-wipes as bought in supermarkets will clean many a surface far better than most dirt removers will — and they don't do any damage. When you think about it, they are made to clean a baby so they can't do any harm, can they?

## Composting

It helps to have a proper compost bin to hold all and any organic waste you can recycle from the kitchen and garden because once it has rotted down you can use it as a base for mulch. Never put what might seem to be dead weeds in for they have a habit of coming alive again very easily. Hedgerow clippings, raw vegetables, fruit peelings, small bits of cardboard, ash from a bonfire or a garden barbecue are all acceptable. Try not to use cooked meats or animal faeces for it will attract rats. Avoid newspapers and magazines for they do not rot down very well. Try to start your compost when the Moon is in Scorpio although Cancer or Pisces will do. The mixture should be "turned" when the Moon is waning in the last quarter in Aries, Leo or Aquarius.

## Cuttings

There are slightly different rules for taking cuttings between indoor and outdoor plants but it would be best to do this in the first or second quarters when the Moon is in Cancer, Scorpio and Pisces — pot straightaway using the same rules.

## Deadheading

The expression is quite well-known but few people know why we use it. Flowering plants produce seeds but once their blossoms die they may well be left alone or eventually fall away of their own accord. You can achieve more blossoms by removing the dying or dead head because this fools the plant and it will actually produce even more. Thus, deadheading is the best way of getting the most from your flowers.

## Fertiliser

It is best to fertilise as the Moon passes though the fruitful signs, that is, Taurus, Cancer, Scorpio or Pisces. For the best results always use a chemically based fertiliser in the first or second quarters but an organic one in the third or fourth quarters.

## Fences

Repair, replace or create new fences in a waning Moon preferably when she is in Taurus, Leo or Aquarius. Virgo or Capricorn may also be considered or alternatively on the day the Moon becomes new irrespective of the sign she occupies at the time. If created when the Moon is in a water sign, (Cancer, Scorpio or Pisces) the wood will rot more quickly.

## First aid — indoors

If you do not have any indoor plants you might like to consider having at least one pot of Aloe Vera available because of its remarkable healing properties in the event of sting, a scald, burn, or a small cut. This is widely recommended by gardeners and herbalists alike.

## First aid — outdoors

Always try to have a few ordinary English marigolds growing somewhere in the garden because in the event of a sting, a scald, burn or a small cut you will be able to rub the leaf of this plant on the affected area. This part of the plant contains calendula which will instantly soothe the wounded area until you can get at something better – always assuming you will need it after using this leaf.

## Fish

If you have fish in your garden pond the water should be at least 60 to 70 centimetres deep. This ensures the bottom part remains cool in hot weather and in the winter ice is less likely to form. Fish are ruled by the Moon or Neptune and fish ponds by Pisces. If or when introducing new fish into your pond, lay the bag in which they come on the water surface for a short while to allow the temperatures to even up. Untie the bag and allow them to leave the bag when they want. It doesn't pay to be too pushy with them at this stage.

## Fountain

Should you have a pond of any reasonable size do think seriously about adding a small fountain or waterfall. Duckweed will not form on moving water. Fountains are ruled by the Moon and or Venus while waterfalls are influenced most by Pisces.

## Greenhouse heating

With power costing what it does these days leave a large candle alight in a safe position in the greenhouse overnight but with the door closed, of course. This should be enough protection from any frost outside getting in — and it is a much cheaper exercise too.

## Guttering

It is quite a large task to clean the guttering and drainpipes so, start the work when the Moon is on the wane. In the long run the clearance work does seem to last that little bit longer.

## Hands

Of necessity hands get dirty after a session in any part of any garden. When you start to wash them always use cold water first. This will cause the pores to close and help get rid of the grime much more easily. Once most of the dirt seems to have gone then use warm — not hot — water and your hands will respond beautifully.

## Hanging baskets

Anything planted placed into a hanging basket of any kind will dry out very quickly no matter how well you manage to try to keep it moist. If you must have one, then line it well first and put an old soup plate or something similar at the very bottom to catch any moisture. Use a better than average moist compost. Hanging baskets are ruled by Venus. If you like herbs but do not have the ground space to grow them separately then use hanging baskets and put a couple or so in each. As long as you attend to the needs of the individual herb they make excellent places in which to be raised.

## Hoses — old and new

Because the old hose won't connect properly to anything think before you get rid of it because this can be a most helpful piece of gardening equipment when used the right way. Cut both ends cleanly and bury the hose just under the surface from one end of the garden to the other (or as far as it will go) without trying to join it up to any existing connection. You may now run an electricity cable (or cables) through the old hose to the bottom of the garden where most folk have their garden shed or greenhouse and enjoy a safe and well-protected power cable connection to either or both of them. Alternatively, put the right connectors on each end of the old hose and when you want to water the garden all you have to do is connect it to your new hose without having to unreel the replacement unnecessarily. These two ideas save time and effort all round.

## Houseplants

Strictly speaking, there are no such things as house plants but in general whatever you do plant to keep indoors they should be planted in the First or Second Quarter when the Moon is in Taurus, Cancer, Libra, Scorpio or Pisces. If you do not like indoor plants you might like to consider having at least one pot of Aloe Vera available because of its remarkable healing properties in the event of burns, minor cuts or insect bites.

## Ladders

Sooner or later you will need to use a ladder (ruled by Gemini) to go up a just couple of steps or all the way up the side of your house. To ensure a firm base especially if you have to stand the ladder in earth place both of the ladder's "feet" in empty paint tins. This will ensure the ladder will not sink in to the soil or slip away. When the Moon is in Gemini is the best time for their use.

## Lawns

To make the most of the appearance not only of your lawn but the whole garden as well you should mow in the second quarter to stimulate growth. To help slow things down a bit more one should mow in the fourth quarter. Lawns are ruled by Venus. Attend to a lawn when the Moon is in Taurus or Libra for the best results. It is worth noting here that a long lawn with equal sides will make the viewer automatically look to the furthest point thus making it seem longer than it actually is. A round lawn makes a garden seem larger while an "L" shaped affair where you cannot see it all creates a small mystery. People will want to see more.

## Leaking hoses

Occasionally, you may experience a small hole in a hose that seems to defy all efforts to repair it. A small piece of wood like a toothpick should be pushed into the hole — but not too far. Thoroughly wet the area so that the wood expands. Put a small piece of sellotape over the tear first then properly seal the whole area with a tight band of duck-tape.

## Mole hills

Unsightly at the best of times these little growths not only spoil the view they also offend. There are two remedies to offset their re-appearance. Cut an onion in half and place one of the halves face down in the hole. Alternatively, put a small amount of used cat litter into the top of the hole.

## Mulch

Mulch is a kind of protective blanket put over healthy soil and is created from inorganic or organic material. Organic mulch which includes grass clippings, leaves and small pieces of wood tends to decompose fairly quickly. Gravel and black plastic are examples of inorganic mulches that do not always break down and does not have to be replaced too often. Grass clippings tend to form a thick pad through which water may not always be able to permeate easily. One should take care to not to use clippings from lawns that have been treated with an herbicide. Gravel pebbles or small stones are much more permanent and are quite effective against weeds. You can use newspaper but it has to be made firm so that it does not blow away at the slightest breeze. Small bits of wood are usually created when you work at odd jobs in the garden. Bark from trees is liable to be found almost anywhere and, for as long as it is reasonably fresh it will be good to use but it performs best when mixed in with compost or well-aged manure. Mulching is best carried out when the Moon is waxing and in air or earth signs.

## Mushrooms

Start mushrooms in the first or second quarters ideally when the Moon is in Cancer. Always try to pick them at the full Moon — they always seem to taste that little bit nicer.

## Netting

You should always spread thin netting over the top of any pond and allow for about 10 cm height above the water level. If you have fish this will help to keep the heron away. It will also keep leaves and other debris from falling into the water. It will afford a degree of shelter for other bird life and any animal life to visit and drink in safety. And, of course, frogs, toads and newts to freely move about as well.

## Paths and paving

If you feel like a change put in a small bend (or bends) into a straight path. Alternatively, if your pathway is straight then create a curve. A cleverly planted bush at such a point is very effective and the change to the appearance to your garden can be quite dramatic as well becoming a talking point for visitors. Although paths and pathways are ruled by Mercury this work is best undertaken when the Moon is waning preferable in Capricorn but never when she is in Cancer or the work will not last long.

## Pests

To destroy pests (or weeds) you use the fourth quarter when the Moon is in a barren sign like Aries, Gemini, Leo and Aquarius. Instead of buying an expensive spray follow this homemade idea. Fill a reasonably sized mug with sugar. Add a quarter mugful of water and bring it all to the boil. Let the mixture cool and settle. Dilute it by about four parts ordinary water to one part of this new solution then spray where it is needed.

## Ponds

Ponds generally are ruled by the Moon and to start one from scratch begin when is she passing through Cancer, Scorpio or Pisces. Double check the garden position you have chosen for too much sunlight is unhelpful and may cause an influx of algae. Use a proper spirit level to ensure the finished article won't have what seems like an irregular surface to it. For best results use a dark coloured good quality material for lining for it will not reflect the light so easily and you won't want to have to do it all again after five or six years. Tap water is not always good for a refill. Always place a pump and or filters where you can get at them quickly if or when they either go wrong or need to be cleaned and or serviced. Pond life can and will suffer if a pump or a filter is out of action for too long because you cannot get at them quickly enough.

## Pruning

All pruning work is best carried out when the Moon is waning in Scorpio but Capricorn will yield very good results for this position will help the cuts to heal more quickly.

## Safety first

Never leave keys in any lock even if you are still in the house. If they can be seen through a window or a glass pane in the door a thief will have all he wants in one fell swoop. He will break the glass, take the keys and, if you have a spare car key on the ring as well — you have lost your car too.

## Salads

Think twice before you plant or sow vegetable salads. Never plant everything all at once or it will all be ready at the same time. Instead, sow a couple of rows of this or that every so often and you will be assured of a more continuous supply. You can start to sow small salad ingredients as early as January if you have a heated greenhouse and use a frame or a hotbed. If you like spring onions and cannot wait until they are ready, chives make an excellent alternative.

## Shelf space

Here is a clever way to double the use of your shelves in the garden shed or greenhouse. Save empty screw-lid jars. Make a small hole in the lid and screw it to the underside of a shelf, put whatever you want in the jar and screw the jar to the lid. The result is a better and fuller use of your shelves. Make the necessary adjustments if you have metal shelves.

## Slugs

These creatures do a lot of damage even when whatever you have planted is under cloches. Use slug pellets or a good slug bait amply distributed wherever there are signs of their existence. Initially a line of ordinary household salt will stop them but the end result can be rather messy.

## Snow

For as long as any snowfall covers your garden and that includes all of the plants — not the trees, of course, then your growths will be largely unaffected. However, if the snow does not cover the plant then frost is likely to attack what is showing. Take the necessary action if this should happen in your area. When you begin to clear freshly fallen snow from paths or drives use salt and or small grit but sweep it on to a hard surface in the garden not a plant area or the lawn for it will kill the growths underneath.

## Spraying

The spraying of insecticides, weed killers and similar materials should be carried out during a waning Moon in a barren sign – Aries, Gemini, Leo or Aquarius. Often, it pays to carry out this sort of task in the early evening for many different types of pests materialise after the Sun goes down.

## Squirrels

It is always a pleasure to watch these lovely little creatures gambolling about but they are pests. If you have bird feeders on poles you may have to move them to where the squirrel cannot get at them. If you really want to upset them pile as much grease as you can up and down the poles. After leaping on and sliding down they soon give up and go elsewhere. For extra safety put largish wooden boards above or under the actual bird feeder. If they do manage to get that far they won't be able to get past this blockade.

## Transplanting

Transplants are best carried out when the Moon is waxing passing preferably through Cancer although Taurus, Libra, Scorpio and Pisces produce good results as well.

## Water butt

In the event of drought conditions applying there are several ways of conserving what does drop out of the sky — especially in April. Kill two birds with one stone here because you will be conserving pure rain water in a water butt connected to the downpipe from your gutter. The butt will have to be raised up so that you can fill your watering can from the tap supplied. Wrap an old stocking around the bottom end of the down pipe and this will catch any unwanted debris from going into the water. There is also a saving here when there is a lot of rain about. Tap water isn't too well-liked by a lot of different plant life for many seem to flourish better when they drink in rain water as an alternative. Water butts are ruled by the Moon, preferably when she is in Cancer but Scorpio and Pisces may also be considered.

## Watering

Despite much advice to the contrary do try to avoid watering your patch too late in the evenings. You see, when you use your hose you will also water the leaves of your plants and, if they cannot dry out overnight, they may start to decay. Rotting leaves can cause a plant to die so water gently instead in the early hours – especially at the roots of new or young plants. Also, try to avoid watering during the middle of the day because water tends to evaporate and the leaves will end up scorched. Oh, and get rid of the sprinkler because it really is most wasteful. Water when the Moon is in any of the water signs, that is, Cancer, Scorpio or Pisces.

## Weather considerations

In spite of the big chapter on weather elsewhere in this book in certain rural areas it has been claimed that it does not seem to rain so much when the Moon passes through Taurus, Virgo or Capricorn. When tasks involving Water signs are required it can sometimes coincide with a rainfall that makes it rather difficult in which to work comfortably. In such circumstances it is quite safe to wait until the Moon transits an earth sign.

## Weeds

Weeds want as much water as your ordinary plants if not more so in some cases. This competition should be stopped. So, the instant you see a weed, remove it immediately, not in an hour or so or tomorrow — but now! Weeds are ruled by Pluto. Weeding is best done when the Moon is in Scorpio but any time will do in most cases.

## Wheelbarrows

If your garden is large enough for you to need one then always buy one that has a ball for a wheel because it will manoeuvre so much the better over almost all surfaces. Try to ensure you buy one when the Moon is passing through Capricorn or Aquarius.